WORDS AND SILENCE

I think poetry must
I think it must
Stay open all night
In beautiful cellars.

Thomas Merton
Cables to the Ace

Sister Thérèse Lentfoehr

WORDS AND SILENCE:

On the Poetry of
Thomas Merton

A NEW DIRECTIONS BOOK

Grateful acknowledgment is made to The Trustees of the Merton Legacy Trust for permission to quote from the verse of Thomas Merton, as it appears in *The Collected Poems of Thomas Merton* (Copyright 1946, 1947 by New Directions; Copyright 1944, 1949 by Our Lady of Gethsemani Monastery; Copyright © 1964 by The Abbey of Gethsemani; Copyright © 1952, 1954, 1955, 1956, 1957, 1961, 1962, 1963, 1967, 1968 by The Abbey of Gethsemani, Inc.,; Copyright © 1968 by Thomas Merton; Copyright © 1961, 1963, 1965, 1966, 1967, 1968, 1969, 1970, 1971, 1976, 1977 by The Trustees of the Merton Legacy Trust).

Portions of *The Seven Storey Mountain* by Thomas Merton (Copyright 1948 by Harcourt, Brace & World, Inc.) are used by permission of Harcourt Brace Jovanovich, Inc. The excerpt from *Conjectures of a Guilty Bystander* by Thomas Merton (Copyright © 1965, 1966 by The Abbey of Gethsemani) is used by permission of Doubleday & Company, Inc.

Sections from the chapter "Fugue Semiotique" and the whole of "Zen Mystical Transparencies" first appeared, in a somewhat different form, in *Forum*, the publication of the International Center for Interpretive Studies.

Manufactured in the United States of America
First published clothbound and as New Directions Paperbook 472 in 1979
Published simultaneously in Canada by George J. McLeod Ltd., Toronto

Library of Congress Cataloging in Publication Data

Lentfoehr, Thérèse, 1902-
    Words and silence.
    (A New Directions Book)
    Includes index.
    1. Merton, Thomas, 1915-1968—Criticism and interpreta-
tion.   I. Title.
PS3525.E7174Z77 1979   811'.5'4   78-21475
ISBN 0-8112-0712-9
ISBN 0-8112-0713-7 pbk

New Directions Books are published for James Laughlin
by New Directions Publishing Corporation,
80 Eighth Avenue, New York 10011

Contents

From the time when Thomas Merton first began sending me manuscript copies of his poems in progress, fascinated by the creative process latent in the variant drafts, I had planned a study of this particular facet of his poems. But, unhappily or not, my plan was not to be realized in that form; rather, it was limited to lecture notes at a time when I was frequently asked to give readings of Merton's poetry to various groups in colleges and universities throughout the East and Midwest. While keeping my initial intention in mind, my focus tended to center mainly on aspects of Merton's spiritual living, in which we had a beautiful sharing, and as a corollary, solitude, his favorite topic, to which he came back again and again. It was on "Thomas Merton: The Dimensions of Solitude" that I was asked to speak at the Merton Symposium held at Fordham-Lincoln Center, at Easter 1970, and I illustrated my talk with excerpts of pertinent readings from his poems. At the panel discussion afterward, it was on his poetry that I was interrogated, which brought my original plan once again forcibly to mind, and I began re-examining the poetry manuscripts in my collection and the taped portions of his latest work, *The Geography of Lograire*, which he had sent me a short time before his leaving for Asia.

These beginnings culminated in the present study, whose scope comprises the entire Merton poetic canon, with the exception of various translations from South and Central American and Greek and Latin poets, which stand as poems in their own right and invite individual study; the "imitations" of Chuang Tzu; and the text of the *Freedom Songs*, set to music by Alexander Peloquin.

Beginning with Merton's *Early Poems*, posthumously published (1971), from the residue of manuscripts remaining after he had made his selection for *Thirty Poems* (1944) and *A Man in the Divided Sea* (1946)—for all of which I have the original manuscripts—through his six collections and last two extended works,

Cables to the Ace (1968) and *The Geography of Lograire* (1969), I have kept to a chronological sequence in tracing his poetic evolution both in technique and treatment of varied themes, as set in the context of his central vision: man's basic orientation to God and contemplative awareness of Him in love in the ground of his own being. This is pursued not as a linear but a cyclic progress, inasmuch as the matrix of Merton's contemplative vision was present in him from the beginning, thence unfolding in his poetry through the simple nature symbolism of monastic inscape, the complexities of its social implications, to its peak shaping in the Zen mystical lyric in which he stands integral and unique among modern religious poets.

In proceeding with the study, where I have felt a special interest attaching to an early draft of a poem or its revisions, I have brought these varied versions into the text; again, where background matter might illuminate a particular poem, I did not hesitate to introduce it, since many of Merton's "poetic occasions" were readily recalled from his various Journals which he was accustomed to send me for reading and comment, and also from personal letters. Besides, in addition to pointing out transitions in poetic structure and ordering of experience, I have chosen what I considered pertinent poems for analysis as illustrative of that particular phase of Merton's poetic development. In so doing, however, I was continually conscious of the fact that comment and analysis, however discerning, can never do what the poem itself as experience can accomplish. Hence, I have quoted at length throughout the study. For the most part, I have confined myself to primary sources, not only because of the presence of the manuscripts in my collection, but because there has been but a minimum of anything approaching balanced criticism of the Merton poetry *oeuvre*. However, in view of the fact that *The Collected Poems of Thomas Merton* was published by New Directions in 1977, preceding the publication of this manuscript, page references to that definitive edition have been added to those in the individual Merton collections. Where unpublished manuscript material is referred to, this has been indicated in either the text or notes.

I wish to remark here that some of the substance of Chapter IV, "Zen Mystical Transparencies," was incorporated in a paper which I gave at Oberlin College in November 1972, while portions of the same chapter were translated into French by Charles Dumont for inclusion in *Collectanea Cisterciensia;* further, lengthy excerpts from Chapter VII, "Fugue Semiotique," were published by the International Center for Integrative Studies in its *Forum for Correspondence and Contact,* March 1975.

Finally, I wish to acknowledge my indebtedness to the Merton Legacy Trust for its co-operation and gifts of translations and new editions; to Brother Patrick Hart, of the Abbey of Gethsemani, who in brotherly fashion kept me *au courant* of new Mertoniana in gift of book or article; and to Charlayne Hays, of the Thomas Merton Studies Center, Louisville, Kentucky, who sent me tapes of a number of Merton Journals which, though I had read the original manuscripts some years back, needed refreshing as to matter relevant to this study. My gratitude is also due to Jennifer Tomaszek, who so generously gave of her time to type the final manuscript.

It remains my pleasure to give a special personal thanks to Barry McCabe, Vice-President and Dean of the former College of Racine, to Doctor Richard Kinch, Chairman of its Humanities Division, and to Doctors James Kulas and Corinna Del Greco Lobner of the English Faculty for their constant interest and encouragement.

Sister Thérèse Lentfoehr
Poet-in-residence
The (former) College of Racine
April 2, 1977

To Barry McCabe
For the spiritual and intellectual ambience
that kept this book alive
and for the "hermitage" in which to write it.

CHAPTER ONE

Beginnings of a Poet

Why are we all afraid of love?
Why should we, who are greater than the grain
Fear to fall in the ground and die?

In "Tom's Book," a small diary kept by Thomas Merton's mother for the first two years of his life, among the March-April 1915 entries is the following:

He said "Aye" in many different and expressive ways, watched and talked to a flower . . .[1]

Let time telescope to the summer of 1968 when, in the second issue of *Monks Pond,* a diverse collection of poetry and "some unusual prose" edited by Thomas Merton, a poem appears by Besmilr Brigham beginning:

The poet is born upon a day
embroidered with one flower . . .
The good poet looks into the center of the flower
where the unobserved seeds are
that grow in his own heart
and he scatters them
with the abandonment of petals . . .

a poet lives whole within a day
whose crest is the one-flower
he teaches men to speak
into the center of themselves . . .[2]

In the same issue, Jack Kerouac, in the first of two short poems dedicated to Merton, writes: "Everybody is in / the act / from the point of view of Universality." Of Merton no words were more truly spoken. And though Merton's voluminous prose writings have tended to overshadow his poetry, it was as poet that we first knew him.

When in the fall of 1944 New Directions published *Thirty Poems*—now a collector's item—it initiated the poetic career of one who in a few short years would engage the attention of an intellectual élite, not only as poet but as one of the most important spiritual writers of our time, or of any time. When the book was published, its author was as yet quite unknown, except for the brief biographical note on its blurb, namely, that he was born in southern France, had lived in Bermuda, England, the West Indies, and the United States, was educated at Cambridge and Columbia universities, taught a brief time at St. Bonaventure College in upstate New York, and was now a Trappist monk in the Abbey of Gethsemani in Kentucky. In August of 1967, adding a biographical note to "Answers for Herman Lavin Cerda" for the Chilean magazine *Punto Final*, Merton named himself not only the author of "many books of prose and poetry" but also an artist, and though living "as a hermit, solitary in the forest"

in contact with groups of poets, radicals, pacifists, hippies, artists, etc. in all parts of the world.[3]

Paradoxical as this statement may seem, it accurately and admirably sums up the status of this extraordinary man, roughly a year before the Asian journey which ended in his tragic death in Bangkok on December 10, 1968, twenty-seven years to the day from the time he entered the monastery.

Merton considered himself a poet, and he was that, and it is highly interesting to trace his poetic development over the years— from the early poems which he chose to keep, to his latest, so-called antipoetry, strongly marked by sociological concern and a richly orchestrated neosurrealist technique.

In *The Seven Storey Mountain*, writing of Robert Lax's visit to the monastery at Christmas of 1943, Merton tells of Lax's taking back with him to New York a manuscript of poems, half of which had been written since he entered the novitiate, the other half dating from the days of his teaching at St. Bonaventure.

It was the first time I had looked at them since I had come to
Gethsemani. Getting these poems together and making a selection
was like editing the work of a stranger, a dead poet, someone who
had been forgotten.[4]

This was the manuscript of *Thirty Poems*. The completed book
reached its author at the close of November 1944:

I went out under the grey sky, under the cedars at the edge of the
cemetery, and stood in the wind that threatened snow and held the
printed poems in my hand.[5]

The collection was enthusiastically received by critics, who
recognized in Merton a new creative voice strikingly attuned to
the tenor of his time.

But Merton had been writing poetry long before this: he tells of
a poem based on Homer—Elpenor falling off a wall—which he
had written in prep school at Oakam, England; and later, while
living on Perry Street in Greenwich Village, he had acquired
what he called "a sudden facility for rough, raw Skeltonic verses"
which "lasted about a month and died." But it was the seventeenth-century metaphysical poets—notably Donne and Marvell,
of whom he was especially fond and whose verbal tone and
rhythms echoed in his mind—that he then began to follow,
though as he says, the poems came slowly, and there were few of
them, verses for the most part in rhymed iambic tetrameter and

because I was uneasy with any rhyme that sounded hackneyed,
rhyming was awkward and sometimes strange. I would get an idea,
and walk around the streets, among the warehouses, toward the
poultry market at the foot of Twelfth Street, and I would go out on
the chicken dock trying to work out four lines of verse in my head,
and sit in the sun . . . I would write the poem down on a piece of
scrap paper and go home and type it out.[6]

But his attempts at publication were mostly unsuccessful, though

The more I failed, the more I was convinced that it was important
for me to have my work printed in magazines like the *Southern
Review* or *Partisan Review* or *The New Yorker*.[7]

The manuscripts of these early poems, some highly revised, had
been kept by a friend who in the summer of 1968, at Merton's

request, sent him copies, from which he made a selection of fourteen, which he had Xeroxed and circulated privately. It was this manuscript that became the text of *Early Poems 1940–42*, a handsome edition with a foreword by Jonathan Greene, published at the Peter House, Lexington, Kentucky, in 1971. One of these early poems, "Dirge for the City of Miami," Merton later published in the *South Florida Poetry Journal.*

A special interest attaches to this early collection in that it shows not only the beginnings of a remarkably free style of writing but an already deep concern for the authentic coupled with the cynical, even mocking comment on the artificial and contrived. "Hymn of Not Much Praise for New York City" is a case in point and, as evidenced by the manuscript, one of the earliest of the poems. There are three versions, the final and perfected one signed. "Thomas James Merton," at the Douglaston address which dates it as written while Merton was still a student at Columbia and staying in his grandparents' home. In sound imagery, he depicts the afterwork hour of late afternoon:

> When the windows of the West Side clash like cymbals in the
>   setting sunlight
> And when wind wails amid the East Side's aerials,
> And when, both north and south of thirty-fourth street,
> In all the dizzy buildings,
> The elevators clack their teeth and rattle the bars of their cages,
> Then the children of the city,
> Leaving the monkey-houses
>   of their office-buildings and apartments,
> With the greatest difficulty open their mouths, and sing:

And the so-called "hymn" which follows is an invocation to the city, ironical and indicting, eliciting a beginning of favorite images—coins, jails, cages—which Merton tended to use perhaps to excess in later poems.

> We love to hear you shake
> Your big face like a shining bank
> Letting the mad world know you're full of dimes. . . .
> O lock us in the safe jails of thy movies!

But the turn of the last lines, though ironic, is of implicit compassion:

No, never let us look about us long enough to wonder
Which of the rich men, shivering in the overheated office,
And which of the poor men, sleeping face-down on the
    Daily Mirror,
Are still alive, and which are dead.[8]

In "Hymn to Commerce," the "dreaming trader turns to stone,/
Because he hears the wind's voice sing this song:/'You shall set
sail from the steps of the Exchange/And word will return, 'Lost
with all hands.'" In "Dirge for the City of Miami," one of the few
poems in which Merton uses rhyme (though he used slant-rhyme
frequently), "all the downcast palms recall/The tears that Mag-
dalen let fall" is of like resonance.

Already in these early poems, Merton is using the "electric"
image: copper wires, polar fire, as in "Dirge for the World Joyce
Died In":

      Rescue the usurers from the living sea:
      Their dead love runs like life, in copper wire.
      Their nervousness draws polar fire of metal
      To blast the harvest of our prettiest year.[9]

One might remark here that in view of the manner of Merton's
death—accidental electrocution caused by his grasping the frayed
cord of an electric fan—the lines and images, as also those of some
of his later poems, seem startlingly prophetic, especially in the
"electric jungle" of *Cables to the Ace*, where it is used as the
prevailing image of our modern world:

      Oh the blue electric palaces of polar night
      Where the radiograms of hymnody
      Get lost in the fan![10]

Also in this selection are poems of Spanish ambience and motif
whose poetic impetus was sparked by a few weeks' vacation in
Cuba in the spring of 1940, vividly described in *The Seven Storey
Mountain*, and which carry the flavor of "canebrake," "traders,"
and the "conga," as in "La Comparsa en Oriente (A Conga)."
where

      Lights fly like birds behind the cane
      And shot flies after, but in gourds,

telling of a shrine to which he went on pilgrimage

> With all the mountain people and pilgrims
> Dancing down to Camagüey.[11]

Another poem, "Song for Our Lady of Cobre," composed on the porch of the hotel on his return from the shrine, is based on a simplicity of contrasts:

> The white girls lift their heads like trees,
> The black girls go
> Reflected like flamingoes in the street.
>
> The white girls sing as shrill as water,
> The black girls talk as quiet as clay.
>
> The white girls open their arms like clouds,
> The black girls close their eyes like wings:
> Angels bow down like bells,
> Angels look up like toys,
>
> Because the heavenly stars
> Stand in a ring:
> And all the pieces of the mosaic, earth,
> Get up and fly away like birds.[12]

The "flying" image was perhaps called forth by the special elation Merton experienced at this shrine dedicated to La Caridad del Cobre, "the little, cheerful, black Virgin, crowned with a crown and dressed in royal robes, who is the Queen of Cuba." In a letter he described the experience:

> It lifts you off the floor when you come into the church and gives you to look at something more incomprehensible, namely a big circle of nothing, a circle that is not a circle, and yet maybe includes the whole universe, but it isn't a ring of light either, and you don't know what it is, except really if you really saw it you would know everything, except for me of course, I didn't really see it but I just knew it was there to see if you could see, only the truth of it wasn't visible or describable in any terms except that it was real. Rather than light it was dark, because it represented a total lack of anything you might be able to see or describe.[13]

When one recalls Merton's later writing on Zen Buddhism, this paragraph astonishes, and carries a special meaning and significance.

In 1944, *Thirty Poems* was published, and then in 1946 a second collection, *A Man in the Divided Sea,* saw publication; the first book, already out of print, was included as an appendix to the new volume. Both contained pre-Trappist poems written between the years 1938 and 1941, together with a number of poems written after Merton's entrance into the monastery.

While still teaching at St. Bonaventure's prior to his joining the Trappists, one day, "toward the beginning of Lent, I began to write a poem."

> I cannot assign any special cause for the ideas that began to crowd on me from every side. I had been reading the Spanish poet, Lorca, with whose poetic vein I felt in the greatest sympathy. . . . Sometimes I would go several days at a time, writing a new poem every day. They were not all good, but some of them were better than I had written before. In the end, I did reject more than half a dozen of them. And having sent many of the others to various magazines, I at last had the joy of seeing one or two of them accepted.[14]

On the reverse side of a manuscript of his poem "The Messenger" Merton lists eight magazines to which he had sent poems, together with their titles, adding: "All these poems were rejected by the publications mentioned—Summer and Fall, 1941."

Of the poems written at this time, one of them, "In Memory of the Spanish Poet Federico García Lorca," evokes the Spain of the time of Lorca's death:

> Where the bright bridge rears up its stamping arches
> Proud as a colt across the clatter of the shallow river,
> The sharp guitars
> Have never forgotten your name.
>
> Only the swordspeech of the cruel strings
> Can pierce the minds of those who remain,
> Sitting in the eyeless ruins of the houses,
> The shelter of the broken wall.

And at its close the poignant question:

> (Under what crossless Calvary lie your lost bones, García Lorca?
> What white Sierra hid your murder in a rocky valley?)[15]

A number of the poems in both collections show an unmistakable Lorcan influence in their chromatic imagery and the alternate use of the quatrain and six-line stanza pattern. All of the Merton pre-Trappist poetry resembles the early poems from which he made his first selection. It should be noted, however, that both "The Ohio River: Louisville" and "The Trappist Abbey: Matins" were actually written at St. Bonaventure's in 1941, after the Holy Week retreat Merton had made at the abbey. Too, there are poems in both these collections—as was "The Minotaur" in the early poems—that are based on Greek myth, such as "Ariadne at the Labyrinth," "The Greek Women," and "Calypso's Island," poems rich in movement, color, and striking metaphor. In "Ariadne," "the lutanist's thin hand/Rapidly picks the spangling notes off from his wires/And throws them about like drops of water," while behind the bamboo blind and palms "In the green sun-dappled apartments of her palace/Redslippered Ariadne, with a tiny yawn,/Tosses a ball upon her roulette wheel," when

> Suddenly, dead north
> A Greek ship leaps over the horizon, skips like a colt,
>   paws the foam.
> The ship courses through the pasture of bright
>   amethysts
> And whinnies at the jetty.[16]

In "The Greek Women," sound images are of its fabric as

> The ladies in red capes and golden bracelets
> Walk like reeds and talk like rivers,
> And sigh like Vichy water, in the doorways. . . .
>
> All spine and sandal stand the willow women;
> They shape their silver bangles
> In the olive light of clouds and windows,
> Talking among themselves like violins.[17]

"Iphigenia: Politics" and "The Oracle" are of like texture, the metaphors fresh, precise, and colorful, as in "Calypso's Island," when she tastes

> . . . the red red wound
> Of the sweet pomegranate,
>
> And lifts her eyelids like the lids of treasures.[18]

Still other poems retain the Spanish flavor of his Cuban vacation, where "bamboo trees click in the wind like rosaries."

But without doubt, the outstanding poem of both these collections, a poem much quoted and praised, is the elegy "For My Brother: Reported Missing in Action, 1943," which first appeared in *Thirty Poems* and later was reprinted in *The Seven Storey Mountain*. It is a quiet poem in which visual and aural images carry the motif of sorrow in simple statement:

> Sweet brother, if I do not sleep
> My eyes are flowers for your tomb;
> And if I cannot eat my bread,
> My fasts shall live like willows where you died.
> If in the heat I find no water for my thirst,
> My thirst shall turn to springs for you, poor traveller.

As they move through the poem, the grief symbols are transmuted to symbols of solace: eyes (sleepless)/flowers; fasts/willows; thirst/springs; and money/tears, silence/bells—to meet in a poignant fusion in the final stanza:

> For in the wreckage of your April Christ lies slain,
> And Christ weeps in the ruins of my spring:
> The money of Whose tears shall fall
> Into your weak and friendless hand,
> And buy you back to your own land:
> The silence of Whose tears shall fall
> Like bells upon your alien tomb.
> Hear them and come: they call you home.[19]

The holograph manuscript of the poem is found in one of Merton's Columbia Notebooks between notes on the Holy Saturday Liturgy and an entry of brief quotations (in Spanish) from St. John of the Cross. It is dated April 28, 1943.

Interestingly, there are also six poems in *A Man in the Divided Sea* that can be dated with accuracy as the first poems written by Merton after he entered the monastery. In *The Seven Storey Mountain* there is this reference:

Already in the Christmas season I had half filled an old notebook that belonged to my Columbia days, with the ideas that came swimming into my head all through those wonderful feasts, when I was a postulant.[20]

Later, he destroyed this notebook but kept the first eight pages with their seven poems interspersed with spiritual notes, the first written in the monastery. These poems, with the exception of one, "The Ointment," are included in *A Man in the Divided Sea*, namely: "A Letter to My Friends" (dated "December 13, 1941, St. Lucy's Day"), "How Long We Wait," "Cana," "St. Paul," "Trappists, Working," and "Candlemas Procession." Perhaps the most memorable is "Trappists, Working," with its opening lines: "Now all our saws sing holy sonnets in this world of timber/Where oaks go off like guns, and fall like cataracts,/Pouring their roar into the wood's green well." As their titles indicate, five of these poems had their genesis in liturgical feasts celebrated during the first months of Merton's monastic life and in the Gospel story. If he was overwhelmed by the solemnity of these feasts, it was the simplicity of the Gospels that won him, as, between the poems on these "salvaged" pages of Journal, in an entry dated February 1, 1942 (less than two months after entering the monastery), we find:

> All the most complicated, deep, immense truths are told in the Gospels but we do not see them because they are all really too simple to be seen. In themselves the greatest truths are simple. Because we take so long in the circuits of our pride to come at them, they seem complicated.
>
> Before I believed in Christ I was incapable of understanding one fiftieth part of the Gospels—I do not say argue with them, I say I could not even hope to know what the words were all about. I say I want to give up everything for God. With His Grace, perhaps my whole life will be devoted to nothing more than finding out what these words mean.[21]

The poem "Cana," though placed in the Gospel setting, is entirely monk-oriented in that it is the monks who speak: "Once when our minds were Galilees,/And clean as skies our faces,/Our simple rooms were charmed with sun."

> Our thoughts went in and out in whiter coats than
>   God's disciples',
> In Cana's crowded rooms, at Cana's tables.
>
> Nor did we seem to fear the wine would fail. . . .
> Wine for the ones who, bended to the dirty earth,

Have feared, since lovely Eden, the sun's fire,
Yet hardly mumble, in their dusty mouths, one prayer.

Wine for old Adam, digging in the briars![22]

Though in *Thirty Poems* and *A Man in the Divided Sea* there
were a few poems that drew their inspiration directly from the
monastic ambience, it is in the twenty-seven poems of Merton's
third collection, *Figures for an Apocalypse,* that he deals almost
exclusively with Trappist life (and death) in a rich and abundant
seasonal imagery of the Kentucky countryside surrounding the
abbey: spring, "When the huge bulls roam in their pens/And sing
like trains"; late summer, when the fields "Frown there like
Cressy or like Agincourt . . ." as the "fierce and bearded shocks
and sheaves . . . shake their grain-spears"; autumn, when he
prays, "Arm us with ripeness for the wagons of our Christ!"; and
winter, when "the landscape, like a white Cistercian,/Puts on the
ample winter like a cowl."

However, the eight-part poem which names the book is different, inasmuch as in it Merton achieves a sustained verse drama
as he sketches an apocalyptic panorama based on a phrase of
Léon Bloy, namely, that the modern world is *"au seuil de l'apocalypse."* The locale is New York City, which in spite of certain
indictments in some of his early writings, Merton loved. In fact,
when speaking of an "incognito" flight there in 1964 to meet the
Japanese Zen master D. T. Suzuki, he remarked that when the
stewardess asked his destination, and he replied, "New York," it
seemed so right.

Using as his *point de départ* the scriptural text, "And at midnight there was a cry made: Behold the Bridegroom cometh, go ye
forth to meet Him" (Matthew 25:6), there is a cry to the Beloved to
come down "and make the brazen waters burn beneath thy feet."
Part I describes the Second Coming in images of light:

> The mountains shine like wax,
> And the cliffs, for fear of Thy look,
> Gleam like sweet wax.
> Thine eyes are furnaces.

And "the mountains quiver like rubber/To the drums of Thy
tread," as the Bridegroom, "in/The world's last night," leads out

his Bride (the Church) "Still fluttering with the ribbons of the cities' mile-long flames," while those who have not tended their lamps, the dwellers of Tyre and Sidon,

> Wet as the wax backs of the hog-hundreds, once, among
>   the Gadarenes,
> Fall down and drown in foaming seas.

In Part II the poet, in a form of responsory, summons the rich women to come to their windows to view what has happened, and has them answer:

> We had not planned to have so great a Lent
> Bind and bite us with its heavy chain!

In its closing stanza the poet orders them to

> Die in the doors of your need, you starving queens:
> "For the vintage is at an end,
> The gatherings shall come no more."

But in the catastrophe Merton is mindful of his friends, and in Part III, as its parenthetical title indicates—"(Advice to my Friends, Robert Lax and Edward Rice, to get away while they still can)"—he addresses them at the "Hotel Sherlock Holmes," the "Fauntleroy Bar," and the "Hotel Wonderland" where

> We swear at the wine as blue as fire
> In the glass of our phony grail.

But while "The dawn bides like a basilisk/In the doors of the Frankenstein building,/And the cops come down the street in fours/With clubs as loud as bells/" there is yet time—

> . . . time to go to the terminal
> And make the escaping train. . . .
> It is the hour to fly without passports
> From Juda to the mountains,
> And hide while cities turn to butter
> For fear of the secret bomb.

The last stanza of the poem moves into an explicit spiritual dimension as Merton exhorts his friends to arm for "our own invisible battle":

> Wounding our limbs with prayers and Lent,
> Shooting the traitor memory
> And throwing away our guns—
> And learning to fight like Gideon's men
> Hiding our light in jugs.

Part IV is based on the text of the Apocalypse 14:14 and closely follows the scriptural imagery:

> Look in the night, look, look in the night:
> Heaven stands open like a little temple,
> With a man in the door
> Having a sickle in his hand. . . .
> Fly, fly to the mountains!

In Part V, "Landscape, Prophet and Wild-dog":

> The trees stand like figures in a theatre.
> Then suddenly there comes a prophet, running for his life,
> And the wild-dog behind him
> And now the wild-dog has him by the ankle
> And the man goes down.

Then in stanzas of reproach to the prophet, interpolated with descriptions of the scene, the poem continues its symbolic personification, "Oh, prophet, when it was afternoon you told us:/ 'Tonight is the millenium,'" and again, "when it was night you came and told us:/'Tomorrow is the millenium,/The golden age!'" Symbolically these reproaches could well be addressed to some modern theorist whose slogans and prophecies are falsified by unexpected and untoward events. In this context, the wild-dog could symbolize history and the spelling out of events that demonstrate the failure of the false prophet's promise of happiness as centered in material riches. But with the rivers poisoned, the sky raining blood, and the spring "brackish with the taste/Of these your prophecies," the prophet has no word to answer as "The wild-dog, with a red claw scuffs out a little hollow/Burying the prophet's meatless shin"—not a pretty picture.

In Part VI, "In the Ruins of New York," Merton visualizes the city after the catastrophe:

> The moon is paler than an actress, and weeps for you,
>   New York,
> Seeking to see you through the tattered bridges,
> Leaning down to catch the sham brass
> Of your sophisticated voice,
> Whose songs are heard no more!

Then using one of his favorite images, that of money, to denote the emptiness of mere material wealth, Merton blazons the city's epitaph in embers:

> "This was a city
> That dressed herself in paper money.
> She lived four hundred years
> With nickles running in her veins."

But perhaps the finest passage in the entire work is the last part of this section in which, after the scenes of general chaos and death, Nature rests quietly and creatively on the ruined land in the peace of a prophetic rebuilding:

> Tomorrow and the day after
> Grasses and flowers will grow
> Upon the bosom of Manhattan. . . .
> There shall be dove's nests and hives of bees
> In the cliffs of the ancient apartments,
> And birds shall sing in the sunny hawthorns
> Where was once Park Avenue.
> And where Grand Central was, shall be a little hill
> Clustered with sweet, dark pine.
>
> Will there be some farmer, think you,
> Clearing a place in the woods,
> Planting an acre of bannering corn
> On the heights above Harlem forest?

Parts VII and VIII are again based specifically on the Apocalypse as the poet depicts the last men standing by the eastward sea where "smoke melts in a saucer of extinguished cities," but fail to see "upon the broken mountains of the south . . . the angels passing to and fro."

In Part VIII, the poem closes with the "Heavenly City" coming down from God, for "there is no more death. . . ./Because the cruel algebra of war/Is now no more." Then, in a final tying together of all strands of the poem in a splendid apotheosis:

> Lo, the twelve gates that are one Christ are wide as canticles . . .
> While all the saints rise from their earth with feet like light
> And fly to tread the quick-gold of those streets . . .[23]

Later, Merton was to attempt a still more ambitious verse drama, *The Tower of Babel,*—also based on a Biblical theme, Genesis 3:1-9—which first appeared in *Jubilee* and was reprinted in his fifth collection, *The Strange Islands.* This will be discussed below.

But the distinctly Trappist poem in the collection, perhaps the most pleasingly articulated, is the season-oriented "Evening: Zero Weather" as it describes a Kentucky winter at the abbey after the evening farm chores are done—

> And the whole herd is home in the long barn.
> The brothers come, with hoods about their faces,
> Following their plumes of breath
> Lugging the gleaming buckets one by one.

And the monks come in "with eyes as clean as the cold sky/And axes under their arms" and

> . . . shake the chips out of their robes outside the door
> And go to hide in cowls as deep as clouds,
> Bowing our shoulders in the church's shadow,
>   lean and whipped,
> To wait upon your Vespers, Mother of God![24]

Effective metaphors of Kentucky landscape where "the low hills lie/With open eye/And own the land like lions," or of the cloister-close where amber bees "wrestle in the daffodils," not only bring these poems alive with color, sound, and movement, but serve to evoke a dimension of monastic living, as in "The Landfall":

> . . . the thin flamingoes
> Burning upon the purple shallows with their rare, pale flames,
> Stand silent as our thought. . . .[25]

As in some of the earlier poems, one of Merton's most frequent images is that of water; sea imagery is appropriate in describing the monastic setting in "Winter Afternoon":

> We praise you, winter, from the deck
> Of this our lonely Abbey like an anchored battleship:
> While the Kentucky forest
> Pouring upon our prows her rumorous seas
> Wakes our wordless prayers with the soft din of an Atlantic.[26]

And again in "The Landfall":

> And lo! dumb times' grey, smokey argosies
> Will never anchor in this emerald harbor
> Or find this world of amber,
> Spoil the fair music of the silver sea
> Or foul these chiming amethysts. . . .
> While from the ocean's jeweled floor
> The long-lost divers, rising one by one,
> Smile and throw down their dripping fortunes on the sand,
>
> And sing us the strange tale
> Of the drowned king (our nature), his return![27]

Here, too, we find the dental image Merton was to use frequently in later poems to portray the industrial world, the "teeth" of factories, and the electrical image so prominent in the late *Cables to the Ace* that point to our age of technology as an "electric jungle."

The critics were not pleased with this collection, nor was Merton. An entry in one of his Journals under the date of March 7, 1948, records:

> *Figures for an Apocalypse* came in yesterday. A child's garden of bad verses. I should have pulled out a lot of weeds before I let that get into print. May God have mercy on me. The reviewers won't.[28]

They didn't. For though they insisted on pointing up a general relaxing of "surface tensions" for which Merton's first collection had been praised and a loosening of poetic line, they failed to note the growing nuance of spiritual vision in a continuum of monastic experience, as his sensibilities, already acute, opened ever more widely to God. This explains, too, why many of these poems have the lift and ring of canticles. The only alternative would have been silence. Actually, Merton had lost no power of image, though he disposed his images differently. There are a few unhappy ones, such as in "Pilgrim's Song": "Breathe us no more the measles of your candy kiss/Unlovely relative!"—and in the same poem, "The flint-eyed brats who own your splendid streets"—though poets today would hardly find them disturbing. Too, in these poems there is ample evidence of Merton's artistic élan as his brush sweeps the canvas with Van Gogh-like color and line, as the sun "shouts and spins his wheel of flame/And shoots the whole land full of diamonds"; or "where the hills of Languedoc are blue with vineyards/Swimming to the brows of the low ridges brown as shells." There is much here that is perhaps too lush and overdrawn, for once the tight surfaces of form have been relaxed, rhetoric threatens to balloon. Though he inscribed a copy of the book to a friend, "I hesitate to sign anything on the flyleaf of a book of which I am ashamed," there are those who prefer *Figures for an Apocalypse* to some of the others because of its simple utterance and depth of spiritual implication. Compared with contemporary writing, one might say it has a special discipline, and few if any could give us poems with so spiritual a texture.

The remaining poems of this collection, with the exception of those addressed to certain saints—Jerome, whose "learned, mad/ And immaculate indignation . . ./Severs our midnight like a streak of flying pullmans"; Paul the Hermit, "Alone, under the companion and untalking tree"; John the Baptist, "You who have brought us to the door-sill of your wilderness"; and Duns Scotus, "Language was far too puny for his great theology"—record monastic events in their locale and setting, either on some Cistercian theme or addressed to Cistercian saints, such as "Rievaulx: St. Ailred," and "Clairvaux Prison," poems rich in functional imagery.

The final poem, "The Poet, to His Book," is an *envoi*, a farewell to his book, the first of its kind that Merton had written. In it he exhorts:

> Go, stubborn talker,
> Find you a station on the loud world's corners,
> And try there, (if your hands be clean) your length
> of patience:

> Use the rhythms that upset my silences,
> And spend your pennyworth of prayer
> There in the clamor of the Christless avenues:
>
> And try to ransom some one prisoner
> Out of those halls of traffic, out of the wheels of
>   that unhappiness![29]

Included in this volume is the essay "Poetry and the Contemplative Life," in which Merton delineates a problem of conflict between his writing and life as a contemplative. Some years later, this essay was revised and appeared in the first edition of *Selected Poems* (1959), with an introduction by Mark Van Doren.

CHAPTER TWO

Poetic Transitions

Silence is louder than a cyclone
In the rude door, my shelter.
And there I eat my air alone
With pure and solitary songs

After his third collection, *Figures for an Apocalypse,* Merton did
some soul-searching, the results of which are at once evident in
The Tears of the Blind Lions, a group of seventeen new poems
published by New Directions in the fall of 1949. This is a transi-
tional book which shows a new experimentation in both technique and subject matter. The imagery is less lush, with a
noticeable trend toward lean metaphor to emphasize the inner
event implicit in juxtaposed images. In nature description, there
is a pulling away from the purely monastic setting: thus, "I saw
Ohio whom I love,/I saw the wide river between buildings/My
big brown lady, going west," reminiscent of a trip to Louisville.
Too, there is one poem, "The Reader," which relies for its poetic
tension on simple, direct statement, a technique which Merton
continued to perfect in his subsequent writing. There is also
much less of the collective "we," as the poet becomes more personal and organizes his poem around the "I" used not as a
persona but as Merton himself speaking *for* himself: "But I drink
rain, drink wind/Distinguish poems/Boiling up out of the cold
forest."

The first poem in the volume is shorter and technically tighter
than those of *Figures for an Apocalypse;* there is a richer resonance in the use of metaphor in the personification of nature in
rain, wind, trees. And the personal note is strong.

> When rain (sings light) rain has devoured my house
> And wind wades through my trees,
> The cedars fawn upon the storm with their huge paws.

Yet despite the storm, the inner creative silence of the poet "is louder than a cyclone/In the rude door, my shelter./And there I eat my air alone/With pure and solitary songs." There is a delightful photograph extant which furnishes the setting of this poem—Merton sitting at a table in a small open hut mounted on cement blocks, which had been remodeled expressly for him from an old tool shanty that had stood in the woods near the monastery's horse barn. Knowing Merton's propensities toward solitude, the young brother novice who did the carpentry confessed to wondering as he went about his work if this was to be the "hermit cell?" Merton was immensely pleased with the result and promptly tacked a picture of St. Bruno on the wall, instead of St. Bernard, which the novice had anticipated. This was at a time when Merton was experiencing an acute need for greater solitude. It was in the shelter and solitude of this hut that Merton could look out on the storm, a quiet which he contrasts with those who "sit in conference" and whose "windows grieve, and soon frown."

> And glass begins to wrinkle with a multitude of water
> Till I no longer see their speech
> And they no longer know my theater. . . .
>
> But I drink rain, drink wind
> Distinguish poems
> Boiling up out of the cold forest:
> Lift to the wind my eyes full of water,
> My face and mind, to take their free refreshment.
>
> Thus I live on my own land, on my own island
> And I speak to God, under the doorway
> When rain, (sings light) rain has devoured my house
> And winds wade through my trees.[1]

Another poem, "In the Rain and the Sun," resembles an impressionistic painting in its movement and blurring of images as it depicts a sudden storm at noon when the sun is brightest. Merton creates a world that has suddenly lost its solidity, and yet the sun shines as the rain is falling. Merton owns his view, he says, "in the air of a hermit's weather."

> Thus in the boom of waves' advantage
> Dogs and lions come to my tame home
> Won by the bells of my Cistercian jungle. . . .
> Songs of the lions and whales!
> With my pen between my fingers
> Making the waterworld sing!

A vivid, almost tangible impression of water, surf, and sunshine—then a prayer:

> Sweet Christ, discover diamonds
> And sapphires in my verse
> While I burn the sap of my pine house
> For praise of the ocean sun.[2]

Though the reader may feel somewhat drenched after reading the poem, he must admit that its images, both visual and aural, are fresh and pertinent, the technique in their use new and controlled.

Another typical poem of this "waterworld" period is a poem to St. Malachy, the twelfth-century Bishop of Armagh and a close friend of St. Bernard. In fact, on a journey from Ireland to Rome (which in those days was hazardous) he stopped at Clairvaux, France, to see St. Bernard, and while there died. As he formerly had arrived at Clairvaux, so now he arrives at Gethsemani for his festival day, November 3.

> St. Malachy, who is very old, gets up,
> Parts the thin curtain of trees and dawns upon our land.
>
> His coat is filled with drops of rain, and he is bearded
> With all the seas of Poseidon.
> (Is it a crozier, or a trident in his hand?)
> He weeps against the gothic window, and the empty cloister
> Mourns like an ocean shell.

Then as the monks "opened the antiphoners/And the wrens and larks flew up out of the pages./Our thoughts became lambs. Our hearts swam like seas."

> One monk believed that we should sing to him
> Some stone-age hymn
> Or something in the giant language.
> So we played to him in the plainsong of the giant Gregory:
> Oceans of Scripture sang upon bony Eire.

As "Rain sighed down the sides of the stone church" and "Storms sailed by all day in battle fleets," at five o'clock Malachy departed—shaking the humus from his feet, "And with his trident stirred our trees/And left down-wood, shaking some drops upon the ground." Merton calls him "the Melchisedec of our years' end," and he

> Who came without a parent, leaves without a trace,
> And rain comes rattling down upon our forest
> Like the doors of a country jail.[3]

This poem, together with "A Responsory: 1948," both from *The Tears of the Blind Lions,* are among the four which Hayden Carruth chose for his anthology of American poetry of the twentieth century, *The Voice That is Great Within Us,* (1970).

A lengthy poem, "Christopher Columbus," is Merton's poetic page of American history. In narrative style, somewhat loose and rangy, but with rich and arresting sea imagery, Merton situates the poem in three time spans, somewhat in the manner of a triptych. First, his coming—"the great Captain with Mary in his sails"

> Who did not discover Harlem or the East Side
> Or Sing Sing or the dead men on the island.
> But his heart was like the high mountains.
> And when the king gave him money
> To go and discover a country
> And fixed him up with robes of gold
>
> He threw down all those pesos and stripped to his
>   champion skin
> And waded into the waters of the sea.
> The surf boiled white about his knees
> And the tides folded behind him. . . .
> What land will he find to believe in, now he knows the world
>   is round?

There follows a quiet passage descriptive of the continent where

> Huge rivers wander where the plains
> Are cloudy or dark with seas of buffalo.
> Frail waterbirds sing in the weeds of Florida.
> Northward, grey seas stir
> In sight of the unconscious hills.
> There are no prints in the thin snows of Maine.

Then, in a Christopher image "the great Christ-bearing Columbus rises in the sea/Spilling the green Atlantic from his shoulders/ And sees America through a veil of waters." As Indians appear with corn and melons, Columbus "blesses the bronze gentry . . ./ Thousands of Franciscans go through the fields with Sacraments." As the poem shifts to a second time span, we see Columbus leaving as "Waving, waving the little ones have wept him out of sight." At "evening, in America's vespers," the dark comes down upon the towns and cities until "there is just one smoke upon the plain/And just one Indian hunter," and the poet asks: "What will you do tomorrow, America/Found and lost so soon?" Then shifting sharply into the present—"Suddenly the silences of the deep continent/Die in a tornado of guitars," and we are in our modern world where

> Bars and factories pool their lights
> In Michigan's or Erie's mirrors, now, on the night of
>   the game.
> (But the bells Columbus heard are dumb.)

The poem's final lines graphically echo Merton's poem "In the Ruins of New York," from *Figures for an Apocalypse.*

> The city's face is frozen like a screen of silver
> When the universities turn in
> And winter sings in the bridges
> Tearing the grand harps down.
>
> But the children sing no hymn for the feast of Saint
>   Columbus.
> They watch the long, long armies drifting home.[4]

And though one might cite occasional extremes in the use of imagery, such as "little fox faces,/Grin like dollars through their fur,/And their meat-eating sails fly down and fold upon your shore," the total impact of the poem is remarkable.

There is another long poem in this collection, "Hymn for the Feast of Duns Scotus," the thirteenth-century theologian for whom Merton, even from his student days, had a special fondness. In *Figures for an Apocalypse*, there is a poem to him in which he names him Mary's "theologian,/Nor has there been a braver chivalry than his precision," adding "Language was far too puny for his great theology." Too, cut from the manuscript of *The Seven Storey Mountain* (because of its length), are several pages on Duns Scotus. Now on his feast, Merton opens his book "to learn the reason for theology," a book

> . . . whose vision is not its own end,
> Whose words are the ways of love, whose term is Trinity:
> Three Who is One Who is Love.

And with a fine theological precision, he proceeds to set in poetic line, free of metaphor, the Scotist Trinitarian doctrine:

> One, because One is the reason for loving
> And the One Love loved. But Three
> Are the Three Lovers who love and are loved
> And are love. . . .
>
> One God is the One Love *propter quam amatur*
> And Three Persons of the One Love are *quae amantur*.
> So to love One alone is little better
> Than loving none.
> But to love Three is to love One.[5]

In another poem of this collection, "Dry Places," there is beautifully placed an echo of Scotus' theology of the Incarnation, as Merton refers to "Adam our Father's old grass farm"

> Wherein they gave the animals names
> And knew Christ was promised first without scars
> When all God's larks called out to Him
> In their wild orchard.[6]

In this book, for the first time there appears a sensitive lyric in French, "Je Crois en l'Amour," with love, in metaphor of the

seasons—seedtime, springtime, summer—paralleling the seasons
of the spirit and the birth of poems:

> Car c'est ainsi que naissent les poëmes
> Dans le creux de mon coeur d'homme
> Et dans le sein de mon rocher fendu![7]

There are two or three later poems in French in the Merton
canon, one of which echoes Rilkean transparencies, another a
brief, witty lyric for Jacques Maritain, based on the parable of the
wise and foolish virgins.

One of the few poems in strictly closed form, complete with
rhyme and a refrain, "A Responsory, 1948," evokes a mood:

> Suppose the dead could crown their wit
> With some intemperate exercise
> Spring wine from their ivory
> Or roses from their eyes?

Though Merton obviously had in mind all the dead, he refers
especially to the war dead of our century, since at this time he was
deeply concerned with the possibility of a nuclear cataclysm.

> Down, down down
> The white armies fall
> Moving their ordered snows
> Toward the jaws of hell.[8]

Another poem in this collection, one that perhaps more than
any other marks a stylistic breakthrough, is "The Reader," a
simple recounting of a monastic refectory scene, with allusion to
the medieval custom of the monks coming in from the fields
pausing to wash their hands in a basin provided at the dining
room door. A vestige of what was at that time a pragmatic
necessity is retained in the Trappist customs, as at the refectory
door the monks stop to dip their fingers in a font. This simple
ritual was the occasion of the poem, though the custom of reading
from a spiritual book during the repast was another. Merton
himself is the reader.

> Lord, when the clock strikes
> Telling the time with cold tin
> And I sit hooded in this lectern

Waiting for the monks to come,
I see the red cheeses, and bowls
All smile with milk in ranks upon their tables.

Light fills my proper globe
(I have won light to read by
With a little, tinkling chain)

And the monks come down the cloister
With robes as voluble as water.
I do not see them but I hear their waves.

It is winter, and my hands prepare
To turn the pages of the saints:
And to the trees Thy moon has frozen on the windows
My tongue shall sing Thy Scripture.

Then the monks pause upon the step
(With me here in the lectern
And Thee there on Thy crucifix)
And gather little pearls of water on their fingers' ends
Smaller than this my psalm.[9]

It has been remarked that in his poetry Merton scarcely if ever
alluded to his priesthood (he was ordained a priest on May 26,
1949). However, in "Senescente Mundo," with its eschatalogical
theme, there is this striking allusion following shortly after lines
of a childrens' play-song:

Yet in the middle of this murderous season
Great Christ, my fingers touch Thy wheat
And hold Thee hidden in the compass of Thy paper sun.
There is no war will not obey this cup of Blood,
This wine in which I sink Thy words, in the anonymous
        dawn!
I hear a Sovereign talking in my arteries
Reversing, with His Promises, all things
That now go on with fire and thunder.
His truth is greater than disaster,
His peace imposes silence on the evidence against us. . . .
Here in my hands, I hold that secret Easter.
Tomorrow, this will be my Mass's answer,
Because of my companions whom the wilderness has eaten,
Crying like Jonas in the belly of our whale.[10]

Although a number of poems in this collection are poems of celebration, as were those in *Figures for an Apocalypse,* nine of them introduce the use of the personal "I" with Merton himself as individual speaker. This together with the simple, stark statement of "The Reader," almost clean of metaphor, point up a break-through in poetic form which Merton was to follow almost exclusively in his next collection.

This new book, *The Strange Islands* (1957), if not ignored by reviewers, received for the most part unfavorable comment. W. S. Merwin in *The New York Times* found in it "an occasional fragment of interesting religious thought," but concluded that "What poetry there may be in the book is beyond my comprehension." John Logan in *Commonweal* became alliterative in his negations, calling the poems "dull, daunted, and reminiscent of Eliot." G. D. McDonald in *Library Journal* called the book "sophisticated, subtle, and uncloistered," while Donald Hall in *Saturday Review* spoke of it as "shoddy, second-hand, and forced." Add to this the fact that none of the reviewers took critical cognizance of the verse drama, *The Tower of Babel,* which forms the middle section of the book, one cannot help but conclude a certain unfairness. Why the diverse negative judgments?

It had been apparent that in certain poems of *The Tears of the Blind Lions* Merton was already tentatively initiating a new manner—poems all but shorn of religious imagery, with a lean verbal structure frequently nonreferential, and with more than a hint of an ironic vision. Here we have it as a more or less general working technique. His subject matter as well is different, as he writes of the guns at Fort Knox (a short distance from the monastery) that "make the little houses jump. . . ./Wars work under the floor. Wars/Dance on the foundations"; of "Exploits of a Machine Age," whose workers are "dismayed/By their own thin faces in the morning." There is the descriptive "How to Enter a Big City," where "people come out into the light of afternoon,/ Covered all over with black powder"; the scathing satire "To a Severe Nun," who has chosen "A path too steep for others to follow./I take it you prefer to go without them"; and the symbolic contrasts of "Birdcage Walk." Merton is already moving toward the surrealistic technique he was to use with such success in his two later major works, *Cables to the Ace* and *The Geography of*

Lograire. And here for the first time is a surprising personal sharing in "Whether There Is Enjoyment in Bitterness," with its imperative "This afternoon, let me/Be a sad person. Am I not/ Permitted (like other men)/To be sick of myself?" This was not the monk luxuriating in great peace and light the critics had expected, but Merton the *man,* who suffered as a man, and did not mind telling us so. Readers were not prepared to cope with this new posture.

However, there are in the collection a few poems on explicitly religious themes, including the exquisite poem to St. Agnes "dressed in martyrdom/With fire and water waving in your hair," and most important for the direction Merton's later poetry was to take, what might be called the Zen mystical poems, such as "Elias—Variations on a Theme," "Stranger," "Wisdom," and "In Silence." In these poems, Merton is at pains to grasp the poetic substance at its ontological roots, then project it directly, free from any technical artifice or verbal elaboration. In so doing, there is always the attendant risk that the superficial reader might not trouble to probe beneath surfaces and thus miss their pertinence-in-depth at both metaphysical and spiritual levels. In a word, whatever the subject matter of these poems, the ultimate thrust of the poet's rare vision is toward a profound experience, and the reader must be prepared to extend himself to meet it.

After reading the remarks of a reviewer of *The Strange Islands* in *Renascence,* Merton wrote:

> As far as I can see, you are almost the only reviewer of any consequence who had a good word to say about *The Strange Islands.* It is too prosy and mortified, I guess. But I feel that it is right that way and I do not intend to get flowery just to please the public. Especially when I don't feel at all flowery any more, I assure you. My life is pure prose, and of the simplest (I almost said drabbest kind).[11]

In a brief preface to this collection, Merton explained that the poems, though standing in no chronological sequence, had been written over a period of seven or eight years, though most belonged to 1955 and 1956. They are arranged in a triple division: Part I, nine poems; Part II, *The Tower of Babel—A Morality;* and

Part III, twelve poems. Several of the poems were written for the nuns of the New York Carmel in response to a request for an Advent "billet," a Christmas song to be sung at the crib on Christmas morning. "Annunciation," "Stranger," and "Elias— Variations on a Theme" are among these, though, as he remarked, the latter is scarcely a carol but represents "what the author had going through his head in the Christmas season of 1954."

In a letter to a friend dated July 12, 1955, Merton enclosed a copy of the poem "Elias" (a first draft), a sustained work in four variations that, as he confided, "best expressed himself at that time." He wrote:

> . . . perhaps you will like the poem, longish, which I wrote this winter. It is the most appropriate thing I can think of for the Feast of Our Lady of Mount Carmel—Elias, zealous for the Lord God of hosts and felled by despair under the juniper tree, and fighting his way on to Horeb in the strength of the Eucharist. I suppose there will be a book for this, with other poems around it, in a short while. I am not making a point of writing poems, but there just happen to be some around that I have written. I still refuse to be a "poet." It looks as if I have to take a vacation from writing altogether, which will be nice.[12]

This poem, a significant one in the Merton canon, opens with a verbal picture of Elias set in a stark landscape:

> Under the blunt pine
> In the winter sun
> The pathway dies
> And the wilds begin.
> Here the bird abides
> Where the ground is warm
> And sings alone.

The bird, one of the symbols which occurs several times in the poem, may well equate with the state of quiet and contemplation, with the Spirit of God speaking within. Elias is asked to listen:

> (Where the bird abides
> And sings alone).

> The sun grows pale
> Where passes One
> Who bends no blade, no fern.
> Listen to his word.

The bird symbol is used twice as a refrain in the poem's first variation.

> *Where the fields end*
> *Thou shalt be my friend.*
> *Where the bird is gone*
> *Thou shalt be my son.*

Elias is then alerted for the "fiery wing," a symbol for the whirlwind, that swept him up to heaven in his chariot of fire, as described in Ecclesiasticus 48:9. "You who were taken up by a whirlwind of fire, in a chariot with horses of fire." The blunt pine, the bare landscape, the seed that has life but must first die, the sleeping stone—all depict a bleak soul-scape where "the bird abides . . . And sings alone."

In the second variation, Merton takes a line from Blake's "Milton" (*Prophetic Books*): "Bring me my chariot of fire," which he intersperses with lines of the poem as he identifies the "old wagon" with Elias's chariot. The whole sweep of imagery is Blakean:

> There were supposed to be
> Not birds but spirits of flame
> Around the old wagon.
> ("Bring me my chariot")
> There were supposed
> To be fiery devices,
> Grand machines, all flame,
> With supernatural wings
> Beyond the full creek.
> ("Bring me my chariot of fire")
> All flame, beyond the rotten tree!
> Flame? This old wagon
> With the wet, smashed wheels
> Is better. ("My chariot")
> This derelict is better.

("Of fire.") It abides
(Swifter) in the brown ferns
And burns nothing.

But "Better still," says Merton, "the old trailer ('My chariot')/
With the dead stove in it," standing abandoned in the monastery
grounds, the rain blurring both it and the prophet's chariot into
identity. And this old trailer, "With the dead stove in it, and the
rain/Comes down the pipe and covers the floor," is by far the
poet's choice:

> Bring me my chariot of rain. Bring me
> My old chariot of broken-down rain.
> Bring, bring my old fire, my old storm,
> My old trailer; faster and faster it stands still. . . .

By now Merton is implicitly identifying his own personal contemplative quiet with that of the prophet under the blunt pine,
while parenthetically the fire-chariot image runs as an obbligato
to the carrying theme.

In the woods that are "cut down" and "punished" the trailer
stands alone, and becomes

> (Against all the better intentions of the owners)
> The House of God
> The Gate of Heaven.
> ("My chariot of fire")

In the third variation, Merton speaks again of the seed hidden
in the frozen ground waiting to grow and bear fruit, unlike the
stone "alone forever." After its second stanza, the original manuscript (dated December 31, 1954) shows some forty-eight lines (six
stanzas) omitted from the printed text. In these lines, in addition
to the previous symbols of seed and stone, is that of a storm in
which the poet is hurled "here, in the high wood/Without a stone
or a light/A corner under a cliff, or any cover/When the world is
run over." Was God found in these storms? he asks, and answers
"no." "Only the wind bullied my sore ears/Only the winter's
trumpet boxed my sides and back/Tumbled me with no bones
broken/Red-faced into the city of the just, half-frozen," but never
forgetting the small voice

> Poised on a clear center, with no thought of storms,
> Always balanced and never turned over, not upside
> Down but always balanced and still, untoppling on
> The One, Other voice differing from all storms and calms
> The Other, silent Voice,
> The perfectly True.

In the Elias-prophet identity, the poet hears the waters tell him that he is a false prophet and admonishes him to go back to the cities because, since he is not sent, they will receive him:

> Go back where everyone, in heavy hours,
> Is of a different mind, and each is his own burden,
> And each mind its own division
> With sickness for diversion and war for
> Business reasons.

At this point, the poem becomes more explicitly confessional, as Merton reproaches himself for being "a man without silence,/ A man without patience, with too many/Questions," blaming God "Thinking to blame only men/And defend Him Who does not need to be defended." Were he to return to his city—"(yes my own city)"—he would be neither accepted nor rejected, since he has no message.

In the fourth variation, there is a quieting of imagery, as in the manner of a recapitulation Merton circles back to the "blunt pine." Then in exquisitely lyric lines, snow, rain, river, the bird, the pine tree tell their own identities and individual freedoms, followed by a descriptive defining of the "free man" who

> . . . is not alone as busy men are
> But as birds are. The free man sings
> Alone as universes do. Built
> Upon his own inscrutable pattern. . . .
> But like the birds or lilies
> He seeks first the Kingdom, without care.

Merton then returns to Elias, with whom he has by now fully identified, and concludes:

> Under the blunt pine
> Elias becomes his own geography
> (Supposing geography to be necessary at all),

> Elias becomes his own wild bird, with God in the center,
> His own wide field which nobody owns,
> His own pattern, surrounding the Spirit
> By which he is himself surrounded:
>
> For the free man's road has neither beginning nor end.[13]

Since the whole direction of Merton's writing, and especially his poetry, is toward that freedom of spirit which is a *sine qua non* of contemplative union with God, "Elias" through its image and symbol strikingly portrays that soul-state the profundity of which no effort at analysis can begin to fathom, for it is ineffable.

Another poem of special interest, though written far earlier (1948) than most of the others in this book, is "Sports without Blood—A Letter to Dylan Thomas," whose poetry Merton held in high regard. Originally, the poem was intended for inclusion in *The Tears of the Blind Lions*, but was later omitted; however, it appeared in *Selected Poems* (London, 1950), edited by the British playwright Robert Speaight, and was later included in *A Garland for Dylan Thomas* (1963), an anthology edited by George J. Firmage, with Oscar Williams as advisory editor.

The four-part poem concerns England, and specifically Cambridge, which both Dylan Thomas and Thomas Merton knew firsthand, and about which Merton suspected that both harbored the same ambivalences. The poem begins:

> In old King George's June
> When evening drowned and sang in the peeled water,
> Hate took place in Cambridge, and a cricketer's death
> Under the tents of Chesterton. . . .
> In this same night of ales
> I was uprooted by my own ghost
> Not without fury and
> Not without cost.

There are references to the "waters of their fen," "seven willow women mad as trees," and the "blue-brown river, bad as drink," where

> . . . boats slide down their oil on an army of wrinkles
> While blades replace the upside down cathedrals
> With a wallop of bells. . . .

When everything went black in the piled city
Pain took place in colleges, and bloodless sports
Under the tents of Chesterton.

Part II evokes familiar places: "the bald lawns," "the enclosure," "the green we had to smell!"

And there the old, whose airless voice
Fell from our England's winding sheet,
Withdrew their leaves, let George and Dragon
Drown in the porter's little room. . . .
But you proceeded to the burial.
Night by night in Camden Town
Up and down the furry buildings,
In and out the boxing alleys, dark as tea
You walked with murder in your music box
And played the pieces of blind England all around the down.

There are arresting images of night when

. . . the men lay down to sleep in the pavilion
With a whisper of flannel and leather;
The ladies all arranged themselves upon the ground
With a wuthering of old fowls:
And now from their ten million pots and pipes
Their dreams crept out and fumed at the wet night,
While they slept in the cloud without Christ.
Then angels ploughed them under the ground
With little songs as sharp as needles
And words that shone by night as bright as omens.

Part III consists of eight tightly structured quatrains of ominous metaphor descriptive of cities:

All the world's waters whimper and cry
And evils eat body and soul.
The times have carried love away.
And tides have swallowed charity.

Bound, bound, my fens, whose soundless song
Both verse and prose have come to end.
It is the everlasting wrong:
Our cities vanish in the wind.

In the closing lines of Part IV, Merton appeals to Thomas to become aware of the futility of this manner of life and the exploiting of his gifts:

> Come, let us die in some other direction
> Sooner than the houses in the river quiver and
>   begin their dance
> And fall in the terrible frown.[14]

From this poem it is already apparent that Thomas Merton as early as 1948 was experimenting with surrealistic techniques. Though later abandoning them for the realistic images of his early collections, he returned to them, and that with a vengeance, in his later work.

The Tower of Babel: A Morality, a verse drama in two acts, constitutes Part II of *The Strange Islands*. It was first printed in *Jubilee*, October 1955. Its symbolism was carefully explained by Merton in an article written at the request of those preparing a TV script for broadcast on the "Catholic Hour" (see Appendix).[15] In it, he referred to the drama as "philosophical," its basic theme "the unity of man in the charity and truth of Christ, in contrast to the apparent unity of the builders of the tower, which was an illusion, the strength of the tower a shadow." Its fall, he explained, "does not cure man of his illusion. Quite the contrary, by means of lying propaganda and false philosophies, the illusion is spread further and carried to the end of the earth."

Three texts keynote the drama and serve as its setting: Genesis 11:1–9, the building of the Tower of Babel; St. Augustine's *City of God*, xiv, 28, which contrasts the earthly and heavenly cities; and the Apocalypse 18:21, 23–24, prophetic of Babylon's overthrow. Throughout the drama, a chorus is used effectively in the manner of the Greek chorus to comment on its action and point up significances:

> Feel the business that springs
> Out of the dark. Feel fear pass cold
> Hands (like wind) over your skin!
> Fear talks out of the thundercloud.
> Ships fold their wings. The almond trees
> Grow pale before the storm.

Not all of "Part One—The Legend of the Tower, *Scene One—The Building of the Tower*" is in verse form: prose paragraphs of dialogue are interspersed as Raphael, Thomas, the builders, the Leader, and the Captain speak together. But at its close the chorus sings:

> Now blow upon this plain you winds of heaven
> Blow, blow, you winds of God, upon the sands.
> Scatter the seeds of war to the world's end.

"*Scene Two—The Trial*" is set in a square in a half-ruined city as the Leader and the Captain of the builders seek to establish blame for the destruction of the tower. Truth and Language are accused and brought to trial. Witnesses are summoned—two Philosophers, Propaganda, and Falsehood. Dialogue marks the greater portion of the scene; then the chorus:

> Grow, Babylon, grow,
> Serve your Lord in chains.
> Chains will be your liberty
> Grow, Babylon, grow!

A last witness, Silence, is called in.

LEADER: Who is he?
CAPTAIN: His name is Silence.
LEADER: Useless! Throw him out! Let Silence be crucified!
    [*Music, an all-out crucifixion of silence.*]

"Part Two—The City of God, "*Scene One—Zodiac*" moves into a lyric and somewhat meditative mood. Raphael, Thomas, the Prophet, and children, who here represent the chorus, stand on a riverbank and speak sadly of the ruined and buried city.

RAPHAEL: Once there was a city where these marshes are,
           Ships at dockside, barrels on the quay,
           Children running between the wheels
           Watching the foreigner's sandal
           Fearing the unknown words of the men with scars.
THOMAS: Now all is sand, and grass, and water
           Where the rank marsh draws one crooked gull
           Men have gone from this place. . . .

PROPHET: The city under the sand
Lives everywhere. It is not a buried city
The westward ships will soon discover
The old city, on another continent
Young and new.

Then, between Prophet and children is a responsory in which the latter, in five quatrains, introduce the signs of the zodiac as they prophesy the new city, the "City of God." The last quatrain:

Washed in silent peace
The Swan and Sirius come,
The Virgin with the Scales,
The wind, and the bone moon.

"Scene Two—The Exiles," which closes the drama, is set in a village on a river. The Ancient speaks:

By the ever changing waters
We sit down and weep
As if we had some other home.

Present with him are Raphael, Thomas, dancers, two villagers, exiles, and the chorus. Then, as if in a vision, they suddenly see a festive village on a river, where there is singing and dancing signifying that "the people are one." The dancers sing:

Once a body had a soul
They were in agreement.
Said the body to the soul,
I will be your raiment.
Said the spirit to the flesh
Now we are a person.

Thomas calls attention to two villages—the one on the shore, the real village, whose houses are solid, and the upside down village in the water, unreal image of the first, whose houses are constantly destroyed by the water's movement, though it recreates them in the stillness that follows. Raphael responds: "So it is with our world. The city of men, on earth, is the inverted reflection of another city. What is eternal and unchanging stands reflected in the restless waters of time, and many of the events of our history are simply movements in the water that destroy the temporal shadow of eternity." Then the first villager:

> In the gray hours before dawn
> When horses stir in the stable,
> Swallows twitter outside the shutter,
> The streets smell of fresh bread,
> And when the church door opens
> One can see the lighted candles in the shadows,
> And listen to the sacring bell.

The second villager:

> Before the sun was up
> We had already milked the cows,
> Watered the horses, hitched up the teams.
> We worked together in one another's fields,
> Bringing home the hay.
> Everybody's grapes will redden the gutters
> When we make wine together, in September.

The first villager continues:

> And now we all unite
> To celebrate a wedding. In this festival
> We dance together because we are glad
> To be living together. We have heard
> The same songs before, at other weddings.
> That is why we play them now.
> We find ourselves made new
> In singing what was sung before.

Then the dancers, in echo of their earlier song:

> Once a person had a friend
> They were in agreement.
> Said the person to his friend
> Take my heart and keep it.
> You and I will live alike
> As a single person.

The Ancient questions:

> These people do not sit together by the waters and weep, as we are
> accustomed to. Why is it that they are happy, while we have always
> lived in sorrow?

The Prophet answers:

> These are the men who have never been conquered by the builders
> of the ancient tower. Because they do not kill with the sword, they
> do not fear death. Because they do not live by the machine, they fear
> no insecurity. Since they say what they mean, they are able to love
> one another, and since they live mostly in silence they know what is
> the beginning of life, and its meaning and its end. For they are the
> children of God.

As a trumpet announces the great messenger, a voice sounds,
that of the Lion of Isaias:

> Babylon the great is fallen, is fallen. . . .
> The kings have seen her drowning in the sea.

Thereupon the voices of the islands, the hills, and the cities sing
that there is no more despair, since Babylon is destroyed "By one
Word uttered in silence." A final responsory praises the Word,
and the drama ends on an apocalyptic note of vision, as all
cry out:

> Lo the Word and the white horse
> With eyes of flame to judge and fight
> Power and meekness in His hand
> Mercy in His look like wine.
> He alone can break the seal
> And tell the conquerors His Name.

ADOREMUS DOMINUM!

To experience the full dramatic impact of this work, it must be
read in its entirety. Preliminary drafts of the manuscript present
interesting textual studies. The twelve holograph pages of the
first draft, and one typewritten page, "Political Speech," show
much correction and revision. Of the twenty-seven pages of

manuscript, there are four of a first draft under the title of "A Responsory (For Paul Hindemith)," typewritten with numerous insertions in holograph. There are also worksheets of a so-called "New Version," dated February 1954; also ten typewritten pages of a later version with corrections. Besides these, there are a type-script with printer's directions for its publication in *Jubilee*, an eight-page offprint dated October 1955, and an article in explanation of the drama.

The Tower of Babel, with soloists and musical score, was dramatized on the "Catholic Hour," January 27, 1957. Further, a special edition of two hundred and fifty copies of the text with woodcuts by Gerhard Marcks was printed in the summer of 1957 on the hand press of Richard Sichowsky, Hamburg, in Garamont-Antiqua type from the Letter Gieterif foundry, Amsterdam—the paper handmade by J. W. Sanders, Düren, and the binding by Theophil Zwang, Hamburg. A handsome book, and a collector's item.

CHAPTER THREE

New Dimensions

Do not think yourselves better because you burn up friends
and enemies with long-range missiles without ever seeing
what you have done

Emblems of a Season of Fury (1963), Merton's sixth collection,
and the first after seven years, presents a variety not only of
genres—the lyric, the prose poem, a letter, and translations—but
innovative techniques as well. As regards content, it is at once
apparent that in the intervening years since publication of *The
Strange Islands*, Merton's attitude had changed, and that im-
measurably, toward the so-called "world." He now found relevance in all that touches his fellow man, with whom he closely
identified, living in the aftermath of two world wars—a season of
social and political unrest and of a deep emptiness of spirit. The
first poem in the collection, "Why Some Look Up to Planets and
Heroes," serves as an excellent example, as it is one of the few
poems on whose poetic genesis Merton comments.

In Notebook #70: Readings, etc., 1963, he writes:

This poem is generated out of tension and ambivalence which
call perhaps for some explanation: they account for a certain tone of
sarcasm and disillusionment. But that reflects only one aspect of the
whole great question of the exploration of space. This endeavor is,
in itself, "magnificent," even in the traditional Aristotelian sense of
the word: a grandiose, noble and lavish display of man's intel-
ligence. And of his courage. The spaceman, if he is indeed the
man of the future, gives us hope for the future. This poem is not
about the flesh and blood real space-explorers who, whether

Russian or American seem to me to be men in most respects admirable, and in practically every way *simpaticos*. But that is not what the poem is about. It is about the image, the fabricated illusion, the public day-dream of space and the spaceman. This is less noble, less magnificent, less filled with ambiguities, fraught with nonsense. It is a front for expressive trivialities, for pitiable delusions, for tragic evasions of reality. The poem is especially founded on this second and less charming aspect of the greatest and most wonderful of all international games.[1]

Its final question:

> . . . Nobody knows
> What engine next will dig a moon
> What costly uncles stand on Mars
>
> What next device will fill the air with burning dollars
> Or else lay out the low down number of some Day
>
> What day? May we consent?
> Consent to what? Nobody knows.
> Yet the computers are convinced
> Fed full of numbers by the True Believers.[2]

This theme can apply as well to the two poems following it. "The Moslem's Angel of Death—(Algeria 1961)" shows the hopelessness of obtaining justice by war, for death

> . . . is a miser. His fingers find the money.
> He puts the golden lights in his pocket.
>
> There is one red coal left burning
> Beneath the ashes of the great vision.
> There is one blood-red eye left open
> When the city is burnt out.
>
> Azrael! Azrael!
> See the end of trouble![3]

"And So Goodbye to Cities" depicts postwar devastation:

> But what is left?
> A pretty little grace,
> (If one can think that way)

Wine of dragons in a poorly
Lighted, isolated place,

Covered with garbage from the black explosion
Wine of dragons and the warming
Old machine runs loose again,
Starting another city with a new disgrace.[4]

That Merton placed these three poems at the beginning of the collection points to their importance and significance. Their theme is also the theme of "A Letter to Pablo Antonio Cuadra Concerning Giants," in which Merton writes that "Gog and Magog will develop the whole thing to its ultimate refinement. I hear they are working on a bomb that will destroy nothing but life. Men, animals, birds, perhaps also vegetation. But it will leave buildings, factories, railways, natural resources."

Only, one further step and the weapon will be one of absolute
perfection. It should destroy books, works of art, musical instruments, toys, tools and gardens, but not destroy flags, weapons,
gallows, electric chairs, gas chambers, instruments of torture or
plenty of straight jackets in case someone should accidentally
survive. Then the era of love can finally begin. Atheistic humanism
can take over.[5]

Another poem of like ironic tenor, "Chant to Be Used Around a Site with Furnaces," deals with the tragedy of Auschwitz and proceeds in the manner of a monotone recording of flat statements spoken by a commander in charge of a gas chamber. In unfeeling, mechanical recitative each horror is recorded.

They waited for the shower it was not hot water that
came through vents though efficient winds gave full
satisfaction portholes showed this. . . .

All the while I had obeyed perfectly

So I was hanged in a commanding position with a
full view of the site plant and grounds

Then the scathing indictment:

> Do not think yourself better because you burn up
> friends and enemies with long-range missiles without
> ever seeing what you have done[6]

The editorial manner, the naked statements placed on the page without punctuation or syntactical arrangement, all contribute to the inhuman nature of the proceedings. The poem was published in the *Catholic Worker* during the Eichmann trial; that Merton had Eichmann in mind as protagonist in the poem is quite probable. It was widely reprinted, including an appearance in Lawrence Ferlinghetti's *Journal for the Protection of All Beings* No. 1, 1961 (City Lights Press, San Francisco). Another poem written about this time, "Epitaph for a Public Servant (In Memoriam—Adolf Eichmann)," is a network of quotations from Eichmann at the time of his trial interspersed with Merton's comment and arrangement; its closing lines: "Gentlemen Adios/We shall meet again/ . . . Without the slightest/Discourtesy/Repentance is/For little children."[7]

In this sixth collection, Merton initiated a technique which he was later to use frequently, especially in his last book, *The Geography of Lograire*. It consists of a mixing of literal quotation from various documents together with his own personal arrangement and patterning, as in "Song for the Death of Averroës," "News from the School of Chartres," and "What to Think When It Rains Blood," each based on a translated text. "News from the School of Chartres" will illustrate this method. In a working notebook (Notes and Readings No. 53), Merton had copied out the brief historical background on this typical medieval cathedral school in which the bishop was required to be one of the teachers. This school had its periods of decay and restoration until in the tenth century under Fulbert of Chartres, who had studied at Rheims under Guisbert, it reached a peak of excellence, with a student body representing Germany and the Lowlands as well as France. Fulbert was a "father" to the students, concerned with their acquiring virtue as well as knowledge. Merton's poem is in seven divisions, consisting of simple quotations (with his own editing and arrangement) from the letters of students and their parents and friends that carry delightful analogies to the problems of students today; they are arranged in free verse short line stanzas. A parent writes to a master at Chartres:

Remember, master, I asked you
To take this child Godfrey, my kinsman,
And teach him in your school.
I ask you for God's love and mine,
To say yes, and take him. . . .
Not only that, but if necessary
He could read in your own books,

And you would faithfully see
To all his needs.

But there follows a complaint:

Now that I am far from there
Word has been brought me: he is shut
Out of your school, and idle. . . .
Do keep your promise—
I beg you to, I beg you.
Farewell.

Another letter is in the manner of a recommendation:

. . . here is our friend Harry.
Receive him kindly, be good to him.
Our clothes
Are laundered in his house
And his wife
Gives us our haircuts.

A letter from a student sounds a contemporary note:

Sweet mother, get the monks' money
That they owe, and Lord Aymon's too
And send it soon with the monk Helyas.
I am having a psalter made;
I need some ducats.

There are other appeals for money to purchase winter clothing ("thick lamb skins"), and also a request for "Father's heavy boots."

Goodbye.
Yes; and send chalk, good
Good chalk.
The chalk here won't write.

The concluding stanzas of the poem are touching in their protestation of friendship:

> Dear friend, be well, be every bit as well
> As I want you to be.
> If you are well, then I am well too.
> If you are content, I am content also.
> Do send me something your Muse
> Says, of how you feel:
> Send by some clerk's hand
> News of your joy at Chartres,
> To Chateaudun, to your old friend
> And say you too are mine.

The very last lines carry a reminder:

> Remember, brother
> To do all things wisely
> And send to me, Aurelian, your friend
> My little books, by this honest messenger.
> Have you forgotten? We studied, as one person,
> Looking together into the same book of Logic.[8]

This poem and others resonate a quaint charm.

As mentioned above, this collection also contains translations from, and a critical sketch of, six poets: Pablo Antonio Cuadra, to whom Merton addressed the letter "Concerning Giants"; Raissa Maritain, wife of the late Jacques Maritain; Ernesto Cardenal, who had once been a novice at Gethsemani; as well as Jorge Carrera Andrade, Cesar Vallejo, and Alfonso Cortes. Each translation is a poem in its own right. (In the posthumous *Collected Poems*, they are grouped together with all of Merton's other translations.)

But a special interest attaches to the long prose poem "Hagia Sophia" (Holy Wisdom), not only because of its content, the "feminine principle" in the universe, but also because of its structure, the Hours of the Divine Office. This has often served as the organizational framework for poem sequences, such as Rilke's *The Book of Hours*, W. H. Auden's *Horae Canonicae*, James Donohue's group of sonnets, *Exile in the Stars: A Book of Hours for the First Sunday of Advent*, and the late John Berryman's sequence "Opus Dei," which initiates the poems in his post-humously published *Delusions, Etc.* That Merton should have chosen this form was logical, since at the time of writing he recited the Hours in choir each day. He arranged the poem under four of the Hours, namely, Lauds, Prime, Tierce, and Compline.

The origin of "Hagia Sophia" is unique, as it grew out of the text of a letter written to Victor Hammer, an artist friend of Merton's, in answer to a question concerning one of his paintings—the center panel of a triptych, painted between 1954 and 1957, in which is the figure of a woman crowning a young boy. There is a holograph page preceding the manuscript of "Hagia Sophia" which explains its genesis, answering the question that the artist had posed concerning the crowning:

> This poem developed out of a letter written to Victor Hammer in answer to a question about one of his paintings. The painting represented the Blessed Virgin Mary placing a crown upon the head of the Child Christ. Victor Hammer said he had no clear way to explain why the Holy Mother should be placing a crown upon her Son. I said that it was most fitting that she should do so, since this represented the Wisdom of God, *Hagia Sophia,* in the Blessed Virgin, crowning the Divine Son with his human nature. After that Victor Hammer asked me to repeat this explanation in a letter, which I did. When he thought of printing the text of the letter, I revised it, so that it became a prose poem in honor of *Sophia.* By this time other personal thoughts about Sophia had found their way into the "elucidation," written at Pentecost, 1961.[9]

The theological substrata of the prose poem is rooted in an ancient intuition of reality which goes back to the oldest Oriental thought: the masculine-feminine relationship basic to all being, since all being mirrors God. We find numerous scientific and imaginative parallels to this intuition in the concepts of the harmony of opposites—the *One* and the *Many, Animus* and *Anima, Eros* and *Agape,* all in the service of solving in some way the riddle of the universe, the secret of the processes of nature. As Merton states in his first letter to Victor Hammer:

> *Hagia Sophia* (Holy Wisdom) is God Himself. God is not only a Father but a Mother. He is both at the same time, and it is this "feminine principle" in the divinity that is the *Hagia Sophia.* . . .

In its most primitive aspect, *Hagia Sophia* is the dark, nameless *Ousia* of the Father, the Son and the Holy Ghost, the incomprehensible, "primordial" darkness which is infinite light. The Three Divine Persons each at the same time are Sophia and Manifest her. But where the Sophia of your picture comes in is this: the wisdom of God, "reaching from end to end mightily," is also the *Tao,* the nameless pivot of all being and nature, the center and meaning of all, that which is the smallest and poorest and most humble in all: the "feminine child" playing before God, the Creator in His universe, "playing before Him at all times, playing in the world." (Proverbs 8)

Hence, Sophia is the feminine, dark, yielding, tender part of the power, justice, creative dynamism of the Father.

Now the Blessed Virgin is the one created being who in herself realizes perfectly all that is hidden in Sophia. She is a kind of personal manifestation of Sophia.[10]

At the beginning of the monograph *Hagia Sophia,* printed by Victor Hammer on his hand press, Stamperia Santuccio (Opus 19, 64), which antedates by a year its final printing in *Emblems of a Season of Fury,* Merton placed the text of Proverbs 4:8–9:

Wisdom will honor you if you embrace her. She will place on your head a fair garland. She will bestow on you a crown of glory.

This text ties in with the question asked by the artist as to the meaning and significance of the symbolism of the painting, and though its final clarification comes only near the end of the poem in *"Sunset. The Hour of Compline,"* it is implicit in its three preceding parts.

"I. Dawn. The Hour of Lauds." The waking to Wisdom and man's being born again "when she touched his spirit" finds its analogy in the state of a person lying sick in a hospital when at dawn a soft voice awakens him from a dream:

I am indeed this man lying asleep. It is July the second, the Feast of Our Lady's Visitation. A Feast of Wisdom.

This was a favorite feast of Merton's which he celebrated in two earlier poems: "The Evening of the Visitation," and "The Quickening of St. John the Baptist." When the soft voice of the nurse awakens him from his dream,

. . . I am like all mankind awakening from all the dreams that ever
were dreamed in all the nights of the world. It is like the One
Christ awakening in all the separate selves that ever were separate
and isolated and alone in all the lands of the earth.

Then follows simile after simile: "It is like being awakened by
Eve. It is like being awakened by the Blessed Virgin. It is like
coming forth from primordial nothingness and standing in clarity,
in Paradise." In the text of the monograph it is interesting to note
that Merton uses the word "woman," which he later changed to
"a gentleness"; still later, in revisions for the *Emblems* text,
"woman" has been replaced three times, and substituted by
"gentleness," "her tenderness," "mercy," and "the eternal feminine," to be finally replaced by "tenderness, mercy, virginity."
The sick man, at the touch of the voice of the nurse, confronts
reality newly and finds it to be a gentleness.

In "II. *Early Morning. The Hour of Prime,*" the poet begins by
addressing Holy Wisdom: "O blessed, silent one, who speaks
everywhere!" and goes on to deplore our insensitivity to her voice:

We do not hear the uncomplaining pardon that bows down the
innocent visages of flowers to the dewy earth.

But when Wisdom has finally awakened the sleeper:

All that is sweet in her tenderness will speak to him on all sides in
everything, without ceasing, and he will never be the same again.
He will have awakened not to conquest and dark pleasure but to the
impeccable pure simplicity of One consciousness in all and through
all: one Wisdom, one Child, one Meaning, one Sister.

In "III. *High Morning. The Hour of Tierce,*" Merton speaks of
the light of God as diffused by Hagia Sophia in the same way that
the light of the sun is diffused in the air that "speaks to us gently
in ten thousand things, in which His light is the fulness and one
Wisdom." This recalls Gerard Manley Hopkins' sonnet, "As
Kingfishers Catch Fire," in which ". . . Christ plays in ten
thousand places,/Lovely in limbs, and lovely in eyes not his/To
the Father through the features of men's faces," and also, as
inserted in the fourth prose stanza of *Tierce,* a parenthetical

reference to the fourteenth-century English recluses who, when looking out on

> wolds and fens under a kind sky, they spoke in their hearts to "Jesus our Mother." It was Sophia that had awakened in their childlike hearts.

And again, Sophia

> . . . the feminine child, is playing in the world, obvious and unseen, playing at all times before the Creator.

She is redefined as the Divine Life reflected in things, and God's sharing of Himself with creatures; she is in all things like the air receiving the sunlight, and the love which unites them. Merton never seems to tire of so naming her. Finally,

> She is in us the yielding and tender counterpart of the power, justice and creative dynamism of the Father.

"IV. *Sunset. The Hour of Compline. Salve Regina*" is one of the seasonal antiphons, at the close of which at that time the Abbey of Gethsemani had its own special ritual. All lights in the abbey church were extinguished except one, directed at the image of the Virgin in a window high over the altar. It is quite likely that Victor Hammer on occasion had been present at this ceremony. The first stanza of the Hour presents Mary as showing forth in her life "all that is hidden in Sophia"; then, in the third stanza Merton takes up the theme of Victor Hammer's query and its answer:

> It is she, it is Mary, Sophia, who in sadness and joy, with the full awareness of what she is doing, sets upon the Second Person, the Logos, a crown which is His Human Nature.

So crowned, she sends him forth as "poor and helpless, in His mission of inexpressible mercy, to die for us on the Cross."

In these four Hours of the Divine Office, the theme moves forward as might the four consecutive movements of a symphony, as Merton posits the "hidden wholeness" in being (Sophia): her omnipresence in all things; her multiple, infinite defining; and her perfect mirroring in Mary. The final stanza of *Compline* presents Christ, a pilgrim such as we:

> The shadows fall. The stars appear. The birds begin to sleep. Night embraces the silent half of the earth. A vagrant, a destitute wanderer with dusty feet, finds his way down a new road. A homeless God, lost in the night, without papers, without identification, without even a number, a frail expendable exile lies down in desolation under the sweet stars of the world and entrusts Himself to sleep.[11]

During a panel discussion at the Merton Symposium held at Fordham-Lincoln Center, New York, at Easter of 1970, a question was raised as to whether Thomas Merton had anything to say about women, to which a panelist replied by quoting from "Hagia Sophia," in which God is represented as Mother as well as Father and Holy Wisdom the "feminine principle" in the Divinity.

Three other poems of this collection, "A Picture of Lee Ying," "And the Children of Birmingham," and the exquisite "Grace's House," which deal with children, will receive subsequent comment in a chapter on theme. So too the four elegies "An Elegy for Five Old Ladies," "An Elegy for Ernest Hemingway," "Elegy for James Thurber," and "Song for the Death of Averroës." Discussed in the next, special chapter are "Song for Nobody," "Song: If you Seek," "O Sweet Irrational Worship," "A Messenger from the Horizon," "Night-Flowering Cactus," "Love Winter When the Plant Says Nothing," and "The Fall," all of which carry Zen mystical overtones.

CHAPTER FOUR

Zen Mystical Transparencies

Closer and clearer
Than any wordy master,
Thou inward Stranger
Whom I have never seen

If the simple statements of "The Reader" and the imagist structuring of "A Responsory: 1948" in *The Tears of the Blind Lions*
gave hint of a new departure in poetic technique, it is in Merton's
fifth collection, *The Strange Islands,* that the first of what one
might call the pure metaphysical lyric appears—metaphysical
not in the manner of the so-designated school of seventeenth-
century poets, Donne, Marvell, Herbert, and the rest, with their
functional emphasis on the "metaphysical conceit," but rather in
a strict philosophical sense, in that Merton deals with "being,"
formal *esse,* the "isness" of things. In this dimension he touches
on what is "not experienced," and yet "experienced," or perhaps
neither, if one may so speak. This delving into ontological sources
unequivocally makes for a certain obscurity, since the poet is
dealing with an entity which can be experienced by intuition
only, and communicated—if at all—through image and symbol.

However highly applauded Merton's two last extended works
(*Cables to the Ace,* 1968, and *The Geography of Lograire,* 1969,
published posthumously) would be, representing as they do the
full development of his sociocultural thought and the stunning
expanse of the imaginative country of his mature mind, it is in
the metaphysical-mystical lyric that he is most truly himself. In
this he is also singularly original, since no other religious poet of
our time, or of any time, with the exception of St. John of the

Cross, has articulated with such candor and utter simplicity, whatever the metaphor, the ineffable experience of the union of man with God in the ground of his own being. That Merton, by his living-in-depth monastic experience, was personally conversant with this dimension is beyond dispute. And those who knew him intimately could testify that, due to both gift and temperament he had, even from his early years (and one need not qualify this by "monastic"), the experience of touching God at the *point vièrge* of his spirit. Add to this the years of contemplative living, with the profound interiority developed in such quiet as was allowed him in a bustling monastic institution, plus the three years of hermitage in which this inner vision marvelously expanded to embrace in a special way all of humanity. One need not then be surprised that some of his best poems should deal with this inner experience. There is a prose manuscript extant that Merton called *The Inner Experience,* a revision of an early work, *What is Contemplation?,* with additional matter added after some fifteen years of contemplative living. Unfortunately, a restriction in the Trust Indenture document stipulates that it not be published, likely because it was not completely revised and integrated into his mature thought on the subject.

This "inner experience" is touched on in a number of early poems, sometimes by a metaphor or simply a telling line. As early as *Figures for an Apocalypse,* in a poem titled "Theory of Prayer," he says to God that we cannot "catch You in our words,/Or lock You in the lenses of our cameras," nor can prayer by way of concepts: "Logic has ruined us,/Theorems have flung their folly at us . . ./Oh, how like a death, now, is our prayer become!" But when these have failed, suddenly ". . . the armed ocean of peace,/The full-armed ocean is suddenly within us./Where, where, peace, did you get in?"

> And the armed ocean of quiet,
> The full-armed ocean, stands within us:
> Where, from what wells, hid in the middle of our essence,
> You silences, did you come pouring in?[1]

And Merton concludes that when "all our thoughts lie still . . ./We'll learn the theory of prayer," which he names a "safe death," a "cell," a "submarine" which few appreciate. In another poem of this period, he speaks of all creation teaching us some way of prayer, "Where everything that moves is full of mystical theology." (This, it will be remembered, was the period of Merton's conflict between the artist in him and the contemplative, an interior struggle which he later acknowledged to have been caused by his having made too sharp a dichotomy between active and passive contemplation.) Again, in *The Tears of the Blind Lions*, in his poem "A Psalm," he makes another attempt to describe this "indescribable" inner quiet and awareness of God as it came to him during the recitation of the Divine Office:

> When psalms surprise me with their music
> And antiphons turn to rum
> The Spirit sings: the bottom drops out of my soul
>
> And from the center of my cellar, Love, louder than thunder
> Opens a heaven of naked air.

Then in an echo of the artist-contemplative conflict:

> . . . songs grow up around me like a jungle,
> Choirs of all creature sing the tunes
> Your Spirit played in Eden.
> Zebras and antelopes and birds of paradise
> Shine on the face of the abyss
> And I am drunk with the great wilderness
> Of the sixth day in Genesis.

But when "music turns to air/And the universe dies of excellence," violent things begin to happen as "Sun, moon and stars/Fall from their heavenly towers." Then "one more voice/Snuffs all their flares in one gust."

> And I go forth with no more wine and no more stars
> And no more buds and no more Eden
> And no more animals and no more sea:
> While God sings by Himself in acres of night
> And walls fall down, that guarded Paradise.[2]

Though Merton had tried hard with words, they seem to defeat him in his effort to express the inexpressible.

However, in his readings in Zen Buddhism in the middle fifties and early sixties, Merton came upon a metaphysical parallel to this experience, which he had already found in its Christian contours in the writings of the Rhenish mystic Meister Eckhart. As early as 1938 while preparing his Master's thesis at Columbia, in a treatise on *The Transformation of Nature in Art* by Ananda K. Coomaraswamy, Merton came upon Eckhart's doctrine of ideas in the divine intellect and refers to him as "a great medieval thinker." This interest Merton was bound to continue in his communication with the Japanese Zen master D. T. Suzuki, who used Eckhart as the example of a Christian mystic.[3] And though in the latter's lifetime his teaching had been looked upon as "suspect," since it did not conveniently fit into the medieval theological categories, he became a powerful influence on Merton, as some of the early Journals show. In Eckhart, Merton found a like attempt to delineate the experience of this inner awareness of God, and he saw parallels between the metaphysical intuition of Zen—its fullness, limitlessness, and utter freedom—and the experience of the mystic. Suzuki's pointing up this likeness was bound to influence Merton's poetry.

In several poems in *The Strange Islands* we find this metaphysical-mystical note. In the long poem, "Elias: Variations on a Theme," discussed in a previous chapter, Merton describes the metaphysical freedom of pure existence. The poems, "Wisdom," "'When in the soul of the serene disciple. . . ,'" "In Silence," and "Stranger" also move in this dimension of pure being, in the sense that they belong to what one *is*, and *who* one is. This Merton expresses in lines of a naked simplicity and directness, using descriptive analogies that can equate with both the Zen awareness and the mystical experience. If in the poem "Elias" Merton not only skirted but entered into this "mystical" dimension, it is in the imagist transparencies of the other poems that he reaches a further refinement of the experience, as witness the lines of "In Silence," a poem of great quietness.

> Be still
> Listen to the stones of the wall
> Be silent, they try
> To speak your
>
> Name.
> Listen
> To the living walls.

> Who are you?
> Who
> Are you? Whose
> Silence are you?[4]

In "Stranger," Merton writes of nature—the trees, sun, rain, the last star all simply being what they are:

> When no one listens
> To the quiet trees
> When no one notices
> The sun in the pool
>
> When no one feels
> The first drop of rain
> Or sees the last star . . .
>
> One bird sits still
> Watching the work of God:
> One turning leaf,
> Two falling blossoms,
> Ten circles upon the pond.[5]

Then, in still more profound quiet, the inner consciousness is aware of a presence of being impossible to articulate. In *Zen and the Birds of Appetite,* in defining transcendent experiences as something more definite than "peak" experience, Merton writes: "It is an experience of metaphysical or mystical self-transcending and also at the same time an experience of the 'Transcendent' or the 'Absolute' or 'God' not so much as object but Subject."[6]

> Closer and clearer
> Than any wordy master,
> Thou inward Stranger
> Whom I have never seen,
>
> Deeper and cleaner
> Than the clamorous ocean,
> Seize up my silence
> Hold me in Thy Hand!

The concluding verse of "Stranger" identifies the self with the silence. In this pure existence "act is waste/And suffering undone . . ./Limits are torn down" until "Look the vast Light stands still/Our cleanest Light is One!"[7]

Another poem, "'When in the soul of the serene disciple. . . ,'" strikingly depicts that poverty and emptiness of spirit in which God can work. Merton takes the Zen and Eckhartian approach, that of *kenosis,* variously described as "emptiness," "dark night," "perfect freedom," "poverty," to which he calls attention in *Zen and the Birds of Appetite.* This poem is explicitly based on Eckhart's *Sermon 28,* on poverty of spirit, which speaks of God as "identical with the spirit and that is the most intimate poverty discoverable."[8] The metaphor for spiritual poverty is found in a series of simple statements as Merton begins:

> When in the soul of the serene disciple
> With no more Fathers to imitate
> Poverty is a success,
> It is a small thing to say the roof is gone:
> He has not even a house.

The "serene disciple" could well be compared to a follower of one of the Desert Fathers or of a Zen master—a disciple who has already gone past the imitation of holy men, when suddenly he has become aware of a great emptiness: "He has not even a house," and freedom. His state is not approved either by stars or his former friends, who are "angry with the noble ruin." Even "Saints depart in several directions." But, the poet counsels:

> Be still:
> There is no longer any need of comment,
> It was a lucky wind
> That blew away his halo with his cares,
> A lucky sea that drowned his reputation.

Nor is there anything left to admire

> Where poverty is no achievement.
> His God lives in his emptiness like an affliction.
>
> What choice remains?
> Well to be ordinary is not a choice:
> It is the usual freedom
> Of men without visions.[9]

It is when we lose the "self," according to Eckhart, "the 'persona' that is the subject of virtues as well as visions, that perfects itself by good works, that advances in the practice of piety—that Christ is finally born in us in the highest sense."[10] This is the pure, the perfect poverty, when one is no longer a "self," a concept that touches the "point of nowhereness, a point of nothingness in the midst of being." As Merton was later to define it in entry 84 of *Cables to the Ace*, it is

> the incomparable point, not to be discovered by insight. If you seek it you do not find it. If you stop seeking, it is there.[11]

The poem "Wisdom" is in like vein as it speaks of "knowledge of nothing," the "void," the "perfect act," the awareness of God within. It must be quoted in its entirety:

> I studied it and it taught me nothing.
> I learned it and soon forgot everything else:
> Having forgotten, I was burdened with knowledge—
> The insupportable knowledge of nothing.
>
> How sweet my life would be, if I were wise!
> Wisdom is well known
> When it is no longer seen or thought of.
> Only then is understanding bearable.[12]

Other poems in *The Strange Islands*, the time of Merton's study in depth of Zen and his reading of Eckhart, articulate this same experience. One might take the first chapter of *Zen and the Birds of Appetite* and match both image and symbol over and over again. For example, in "In Silence,"

> . . . The whole
> World is secretly on fire. The stones
> Burn, even the stones
> They burn me. How can a man be still or
> Listen to all things burning? How can he dare
> To sit with them when
> All their silence
> Is on fire?[13]

In the essay "The Study of Zen," Merton writes: "But there eventually comes a time when like Moses we see that the thornbush of cultural and religious forms is suddenly on fire and we are summoned to approach it without shoes—and probably without feet. Is the fire other than the Bush? More than the Bush? Or is it more the Bush than the Bush itself?"[14]

In *Emblems of a Season of Fury* are several poems of like texture, though in some of them Merton speaks of "solitude" as "going before you into emptiness" and of a paradise in you "that is no place," to enter which is "to become unnameable."

> Whoever is there is homeless for he has no door and
>   no identity with which to go out and to come in.
>
> Whoever is nowhere is nobody, and therefore cannot
>   exist except as unborn:
> No disguise will avail him anything
>
> Such a one is neither lost nor found.[15]

"A Messenger from the Horizon" depicts the limitless freedom of one in whom God takes "inexhaustible creative delight." In an image analogous to Eckhart's simile of a horse "let loose over a green heath . . . to gallop as a horse will, as fast as he can over the greensward," Merton remarks that "as an expression of insight into the very core of life, it is incomparable." In the poem, he presents

> . . . a naked runner
> A messenger,
> Following the wind
> From budding hills. . . .
> Silence is his way.
>
> Rain is his own
> Most private weather.
> Amazement is his star.

Then the reader is asked to

> Pardon all runners. . . .
> Pardon their impulses,

Their wild attitudes,
Their young flights, their reticence.

When a message has no clothes on
How can it be spoken?[16]

The ineffableness of the mystic experience. "Love Winter When the Plant Says Nothing" is yet another example:

O little forests, meekly
Touch the snow with low branches!
O covered stones
Hide the house of growth! . . .

Pray undistracted
Curled tree
Carved in steel—
Buried zenith!

Fire, turn inward
To your weak fort,
To a burly infant spot,
A house of nothing.

O peace, bless this mad place:
Silence, love this growth.

O silence, golden zero
Unsetting sun

Love winter when the plant says nothing.[17]

A like atmosphere is evoked in "O Sweet Irrational Worship," in which "ceasing to question the sun/I have become light/Bird and wind."

Out of my grass heart
Rises the bobwhite.

Out of my nameless weeds
His foolish worship.[18]

There are three other poems as well which approach this rarified atmosphere: "Night-Flowering Cactus," "Song: If You Seek. . . ," and "The Fall," though there is more working in words among the images. The night-flowering cactus knows its time, "which is

obscure, silent and brief/For I am present without warning one
night only."

> He who sees my purity
> Dares not speak of it.
> When I open once for all my impeccable bell
> No one questions my silence:
> The all-knowing spirit of night flies out of my mouth.
>
> Have you seen it? Even though my mirth has
>   quickly ended
> You live forever in its echo:
> You will never be the same again.[19]

Merton here attempts to describe the "perfect act" that is "empty"
(which he goes into some detail to define in entry 37 of *Cables to
the Ace*), using the night-flowering cactus flower as symbol of
this Zen consciousness, "my timeless moment of void." It serves as
well the Eckhartian concept of "perfect poverty" that occurs only
when there is no self left as a "place" for God to act in, and hence
He acts purely in Himself. It is only then that one comes to his
"true self" or, in Zen terms, the "no-self," in which one achieves
his true identity which consists in "the birth of Christ in us."
Variously described as this state may be, it also equates with the
"darkness" of the apophatic mystic St. John of the Cross—"The
all-knowing bird of night flies out of my mouth"—an experience
that cannot be seen. The cactus's moment of bloom is a "timeless
moment," and though its moment of joy (of birth) ends quickly,
yet one who has experienced it lives "forever in its echo:/You will
never be the same again."

In "Song: If you Seek. . . ," a poem that Merton had lettered
on the dust-jacket of the special edition of *The Solitary Life*,
printed on the hand press of Victor Hammer (1960), one is invited
into an "inner solitude" where "If you seek a heavenly light/I,
Solitude, am your professor!" Throughout the poem as Solitude
speaks, one is aware of the same quiet and stillness, the emptiness
of that "perfect act" which Merton has been so much at pains to
articulate. "I go before you into emptiness," says Solitude, into
that inner place, "your innermost apartment."

> I am the appointed hour,
> The "now" that cuts
> Time like a blade.
>
> I am the unexpected flash
> Beyond "yes," beyond "no,"
> The forerunner of the Word of God.

And if Solitude be followed, the disciple will be led "To golden-haired suns,/Logos and music, blameless joys,/Innocent of questions/And beyond answers:"

> For I, Solitude, am thine own self:
> I, Nothingness, am thy All.
> I, Silence, am thy Amen![20]

In "The Fall," Merton tries once again to describe the indescribable "still point of the spirit":

> There is no where in you a paradise that is no place
>   and there
> You do not enter except without a story.[21]

There are striking parallels as well in sections 37, 38, and 84 of *Cables to the Ace*, as Merton tries one way and another to describe the "empty act," the awareness of the inner Presence in which one is *one* with that Presence, for, "to enter there is to become unnameable."

> Whoever is nowhere is nobody, and therefore cannot
>   exist except as unborn. . . .

Here again is the Zen echo in section 38 of *Cables to the Ace:*

> Follow the ways of no man, not even your own. The way that is
> most yours is no way. For where are you? Unborn! Your way
> therefore is unborn.[22]

After manipulating image after image and symbol after symbol in an attempt to express the inexpressible, Merton perhaps succeeds best in "Song for Nobody," wherein

> A yellow flower
> (Light and spirit)
> Sings by itself
> For nobody.

The pure essence of existence—and he asks that it be not disturbed, nor should anyone "touch this gentle sun/In whose dark eye/Someone is awake," the God-presence in the simple being in which there is

> (No light, no gold, no name, no color
> And no thought:
> O, wide awake!)
>
> A golden heaven
> Sings by itself
> A song to nobody.[23]

In sum—and that not excluding Merton's two last extended and diversely structured works, *Cables to the Ace* and *The Geography of Lograire*, which are ample evidence of the vast areas of his concern joined to a skill in formal organization—one is tempted to conclude that Merton's unique gift declares itself unmistakably in the poetic contours of the metaphysical lyric. In these he is pre-eminently himself as poet and mystic, as he tries to capture in image and symbol the ineffable experience of God—an experience which he *lived* and which formed the matrix of those areas of social concern so evident in his last two extended works. The truth of this conclusion is the more emphasized by the fact that in the final manuscript of *Cables to the Ace*, even though the poem had already enacted itself as an artistic and deeply human artifact, as a last gesture he chose to pull its total focus into a Zen mystical dimension by the addition of specific texts from Eckhart, Ruysbroeck, Dögen, and his own personal commentary on the Zen mystical experience.

CHAPTER FIVE

Surrealistic Patternings

Believe yourselves
Arguments of a speechless
God lost in the
City of squares
Out of a job again and looking
For his arm

To enter the country of Merton's later poems is to experience a new poetic climate. There are roughly fifty poems, of which about half were first published in scattered magazines, that have now been gathered in *The Collected Poems of Thomas Merton*.[1] These present a wide variety of subject matter, also of techniques. There are lyrics of metaphysical texture, imagist and surrealist poems, many of ironic thrust, and a few of a delightful whimsy, such as "Les Cinq Vièrges," written as gift to the late Jacques Maritain, and the longish "Western Fellow Students Salute with Calypso Anthems the Movie Career of Robert Lax" for his friend of Columbia days who had been in a movie in Greece. Nor was Merton above a witty exercise, "bbbbbbbbbb: (trying out a new ribbon!!)"

One of the earliest of these poems, and one of the finest, is "Paper Cranes," referring to the Japanese peace symbol, later published in *Prelude 27* (1966) and translated into Japanese by one of the victims of Hiroshima, who in May 1964, while on a Peace Pilgrimage, visited Merton at Gethsemani. The poem, however, had been completed before the pilgrims' arrival, though in anticipation of their visit, and Merton read it on that occasion. Its brief, eighteen lines contrast the symbols of dove and hawk, the manuscripts showing three slightly revised drafts, the final revision carrying the added title "(The Hibakusha come to the Abbey of Gethsemani)." The poem must be read in its entirety:

> How can we tell a paper bird
> Is stronger than a hawk
> When it has no metal for talons?
> It needs no power to kill
> Because it is not hungry.
>
> Wilder and wiser than eagles
> It ranges round the world
> Without enemies
> And free of cravings.
>
> The child's hand
> Folding these wings
> Wins no wars and ends them all.
>
> Thoughts of a child's heart
> Without care, without weapons!
> So the child's eye
> Gives life to what it loves
> Kind as the innocent sun
> And lovelier than all dragons![2]

Merton later spoke of how deeply touched he was when on leaving hermitage, one of the pilgrims, a quiet, silent woman, came up to his table and smilingly laid a folded paper crane upon it.

Three poems written at about this time (1963–64) deal with an event in the lives of three historic personages: "Seneca," the stoic philosopher; "Origen," the Greek philosopher and Church Father; and "St. Maedoc—Fragment of an Ikon," the Irish legendary miracle-worker—in each of which Merton achieves a marked poetic objectivity. "Seneca," is a gentle poem in which, line by line, Merton sketches a portrait of the Roman philosopher's wife who, "When the torch is taken/And the room is dark," waits up for him "Knowing Seneca's ways." Meanwhile "her wise/Lord promenades/Within his own temple/Master and censor/Overseeing/His own ways." At this point the manuscript of the poem makes explicit that such was Seneca's wont at night—to search his own soul—as he walked "in the Templehouse of spirit/ Finding out/This day's self/His own self-ways/With his secret lamp" . . . in his own "inner city."[3] With its closing lines the poem depicts him

> With his philosophical sconce
> Policing the streets
> Of this secret Rome
> While the wife
> Silent as a sea
> Policing nothing
> Waits in darkness
> For the Night Bird's
> Inscrutable Cry.[4]

Rather unusual with Merton are the short lines which describe through action—a simple incident, a fragment of life dramatized.

The poem on Origen (controversial in his lifetime because of his doctrine), encompasses a history. "His sin was to speak first/ Among mutes. Learning/Was heresy," and it was Rufinus "Awake in his Italian room" who "Lit this mad lighthouse, *beatus/ignis amoris* for the whole West." Those who admired him, "gave him names/Of gems or metals:—'Adamant.' Jerome/Said his guts were brass;/But having started with this pretty/Word he changed, another time,/To hatred." But it was the Greeks who "destroyed their jewel/For 'frightful blasphemy'"—

> Since he had said hell-fire
> Would at last go out
> And all the damned repent.

Even Bede, "Otherwise a gentle thinker," condemned him; so too pontiffs, but

> In the end, the medieval West
> Would not renounce him. All antagonists,
> Bernards and Abelards together, met in this
> One madness for the sweet poison
> Of compassion in this man
> Who thought he heard all beings
> From stars to stones, angels to elements, alive
> Crying for the Redeemer with a live grief.[5]

Evocative of the cosmic vision of a Duns Scotus or a Teilhard de Chardin.

"St. Maedoc—Fragment of an Ikon" moves by connotative links between images, and it is conjecture as to whether or not the poem is based on a real ikon fragment—Merton's hermitage was hung with ikons—or whether it is used as a symbol of an incident in St. Maedoc's life. He was Bishop of Ferns, Ireland, and legends are inlaid with his working of wonders, though hagiographers have shown him practical as well, as when departing to study Scripture under St. David in Wales, and knowing the abstemious habits of David's monks, he took along "a carload of beer." The poem is built about his confrontation with an embattled king:

> Maedoc of the floating stone
> Of the fresh hazel
> Son of a star
>
> Bells will ring where
> The wolves were
> Ath Ferna
> Of the green shore
>
> Like sunlight in spring rain
> Maedoc and his monks
> Come through the wood
> To the King's rock

Then images of battle—"Water and Spirit/Bright wave and flame/At the wood's edge," but Maedoc's sign (the cross) halted the king's army and he fled:

> No fighting the saints
> The Blessed Trinity
> Or Maedoc's wonders.

The concluding stanza tells how "Aed Duv son of Fergus/With a face like a board/Prayed and slept/In Maedoc's cowl/For a hideous man/A new fair form/A New Name/Without despair."[6]

In Merton's originally planned Part II of *Cables to the Ace*, he placed first a very personal poem titled "With the World in My Blood Stream"—ninety-seven lines composed in early 1966, and only slightly revised. The fact that he placed it first points to its singular importance. When Merton retired to the hermitage in the fall of 1965, he did so in a spirit of openness to all beings. His *mythos* of concern was a world now seen in a perspective that only a solitude lived in and for God could make possible. The poem's locale is a hospital in which Merton was a patient. Mixed in with the almost clinical overtones of the poem is the strong theological note of his identity with Christ in his suffering, as the images move in a maze of sounds that mingle in his mind: "the musical machinery/All around overhead/Play upon my metal system/My invented backbone/Lends to the universal tone/A flat impersonal song." He wonders who he is:

> Thanks to this city
> I am still living
> But whose life lies here
> And whose invented music sings?

And though "Bleeding in a numbered bed/. . . all my veins run/With Christ and with the stars' plasm." Then the almost hallucinatory lines:

> Ancestors and Indians
> Zen Masters and Saints
> Parade in the incredible hotel
> And dark eyed Negro mercy bends
> The uncertain fibres of the will
> Toward recovery and home.
> I have no more sweet home
> I doubt the bed here and the road there
> And WKLO I most abhor
> My head is rotten with the town's song.

Here depicted in all its starkness is the suffering of a man in more than physical pain, hungry not only in body but in mind, not only for "invented air" but more "for the technical community of men/For my lost Zen breathing." He experiences in himself "man's enormous want"—

> Until the want itself is gone
> Nameless bloodless and alone
> The Cross comes and Eckhart's scandal
> The Holy Supper and the precise wrong.

And the accurate little spark
In emptiness in the jet stream
. . . .
A lost spark in Eckhart's Castle. . . .

Only the spark is now true
Dancing in the empty room
All around overhead
While the frail body of Christ
Sweats in a technical bed
I am Christ's lost cell
His childhood and desert age
His descent into hell.

Love without need and without name
Bleeds in the empty problem
And the spark without identity
Circles the empty ceiling.[7]

A final version of this poem, is dated April 1966, was published in *Florida Quarterly* (Summer 1967) and later included in *Sensation Time at the Home,* brought out posthumously in an appendix to the *Collected Poems.* But there was an earlier version, slightly shorter, whose ending was:

And love without need without name
Without answer without problem
Love is the way and love is home.

This is perhaps Merton's most poignant and anguished poem. In another, "The Lion," written about the same time, he speaks of the lion as it climbs into the dark (Merton's view of the stars from the hermitage hill was breathtaking)—and he is moved to comparison with his own soul state:

But in the low regions
Of my planetary blood
There is nothing magnificent
Not stars but glistening points
Of exasperation
I am a blind man dazzled
By nerves and fireflies.

Again, in lines punctuated by the same sense of frustration and malaise (in part, easily an aftermath of his illness), the metaphor is unmistakable:

> If I once had a wagon of lights to ride in
> The axel is broken
> The horses are shot.
>
> And it does not really matter
> I have arrived
> Wounded with unimportance
> At the end of my stale journey
> Ashamed of being so tired.[8]

This was indeed a part of Merton's *kenosis,* his "dark night."

"Early Blizzard," a quiet lyric, and another very personal poem, evokes a mood of peace in solitude, as Merton writes, "It feels good to be without hearing/In the lone house/Loaded and warm"—

> Or out following the hidden ways
> The ways of instinct
> A stranger in the double
> Loneliness of snow.

As he walks silently "Ploughing the deep drifts," he goes "knee deep in silence/Where the storm smokes and stings/The chattering leaves," which cannot be ruled or told where to go. Finally, he admonishes himself to

> Sink in the hidden wood
> And let the weather
> Be what it is
>
> Let seasons go
> Far wrong
> Let freedom sting
> The glad wet eye
> Of winter.[9]

Another exceptional lyric, one of the group intended for inclusion in the planned second section of *Cables to the Ace,* is "Rilke's Epitaph." At the time of its writing, Merton was engaged in an intensive study of Rilke's *Duino Elegies* and *Sonnets to Orpheus,* copies of which he had asked to be sent to him by James Laughlin of New Directions in the J. B. Leishman translation. This study was helped by critical readings from Nishida Katori, the Japanese philosopher, and Romano Guardini. Though Merton realized he would never be a poet in Rilke's sense, he was much impressed by the latter's thoughts on death and on the pure event, which could be valid for his own life. The rose-imagery of the poem derives from Rilke's "The Gazelle: Dorcas Gazelle," out of whose forehead "leaf and lyre climb,/and all you are has been in simile/passing through those love-songs continually/whose words will cover, light as leaves of rose,/the no-more-reader's eyes, which he will close,"[10] and Rilke's epitaph, which Merton quotes as the first verse of his poem, with very slight changes from the Leishman translation:

> *"Rose, O pure*
> *Contradiction*
> *Longing to be nobody's*
> *Sleep under so many*
> *Lids."*

> Pierced by an innocent
> Rose, (O pure
> Contradiction)
> Nobody's lids
> And everybody's sleep

> Death (nothing but distance
> And unreason)
> You accept it,
> You pluck it.

> *Music, (O pure*
> *Contradiction*
> *Everybody's*
> *Vision.*[11]

The poem's effect is lapidary in its juxtaposed image and symbol: the rose/death/"everybody's sleep . . ./You accept it,/You pluck it." The "pure contradiction" is used in the sense of Nishida, who considered it the value of life—a state of productive contradiction—working with and against the elements that equate with "active intuition." In the concluding stanza, "music" is a symbol of *"Everybody's/Vision."*

Another poem in the same imagist manner is the French "Le Secret," which "occurred," as he wrote to a friend, "all of a sudden one morning about 4 A.M. (January 23, 1966) in a time of pre-dawn darkness," which Merton loved and found perfect for prayer and reading. The poem is written in fourteen short quatrains, for the most part in four-syllable count, and tightly rhymed:

> Puisque je suis
> Imaginaire
> La belle vie
> M'est familiere,
>
> Et je m'en vais
> Sur un nuage
> Faire un serein
> Petit voyage.

(In an entry in a personal Journal, under date of January 23, 1966, Merton gives an English translation of the poem from which the translated lines used here are taken.)

The trip he charts in the poem is not a short one, and he writes that were the reader told his secrets, he would laugh. He then moves swiftly into a paradox of the inner self: "Mon coeur est nu/Qui rien ne cache/Et rien ne garde/Qu'il ne lâche" ("My heart is naked/and hides nothing,/and keeps nothing/without letting it go").

> Et mes deux yeux
> Sont mappemondes
> Tout je vois
> Et rien ne gronde.

Then "J'étais en Chine," where he saw great happiness, and again ". . . au centre/De la terre" "where there was no misery." And should he visit the planets, he goes on to say, and the secret stars in the darkest night—"Je suis personne/Et tout le monde" ("I am nobody/and everybody"). And should he leave without remembering, "Comment pourrai-je/Revenir?" ("How should I return?"). Merton then asks that he be not looked for on his return, for "Je serai là/Sans le savoir" ("I shall be there/without knowing it"). And he tells how in the two concluding stanzas:

> Sans figure
> Et sans nom
> Sans reputation
> Ni renom,
>
> Je suis un oiseau
> Enchante
> Amour que Dieu
> A invente.[12]

He will return without form, name, reputation, or renown, for "I am an enchanted/bird: Love which God/has found." A lyric that is sheer magic, and one of the most perfect poems Merton has written, paced as it is in his "native" French (he was born in Prades in the Pyrenees and even as a child was bilingual, though his dialect was Catalan).

"The Night of Destiny," which celebrates the close of the Moslem fast of Ramadan and the giving of the Koran to Mohammed, seemed to Merton to partake of the spirit of Christmas "when the heavens open and the 'Word' is heard on earth." The poem in a number of the lines also touches on the Zen emptiness:

> My love is darkness!
>
> Only in the Void
> Are all ways one:
>
> Only in the night
> Are all the lost
> Found.
>
> In my ending is my meaning.[13]

The last line is identical with the poem's opening line—an envelope style which Merton rarely used—in which the repetition at the poem's close gives it a gathered richness of meaning because of the lines between. Of this feast, Merton remarked in a Journal that he stayed up all night because of it, likening it to a Moslem

Christmas, "Heaven open to earth, the angels and the Spirits come down, all the prayers of the faithful are answered, night of joy and peace." He shared in the Moslems' joy, prayed for them, for his own needs, and for peace.

Then there are the more recent poems, surrealist, or more correctly neosurrealist, a technique with which Merton experimented with more or less success for the last three or four years of his life and which coincided roughly with the beginnings of *Cables to the Ace.* Some of these poems in content tie in with an event in the external world, and though Merton may retain a conventional syntax, the metaphors tend to drift loose from their referents, with the result of a suspension of meaning and a certain amount of obscurity. This is where the reader must involve himself and do some creating on his own; after all, the logical meaning of a poem is only one of the components of the total poetic experience.

"A Round and a Hope for Smithgirls" is an example in which no event is specifically cited, and begins:

> Children the time of angry Fathers
> Is torn off the calendar
> They turn to shadows in the spring
>
> The city that they thought was theirs
> They surrender to the gentle
> Children that were
> Made unhappy in the electric flood
> And emptiness.

A number of interpretations might be given to the above lines—it could refer to a state of things in which true religious experience had been lost in ritualistic formality. Merton exhorts the children to "Believe in him alone/The gentle One/You yourselves are," thus identifying them with Christ, and asking them to

> Believe yourselves
> Arguments of a speechless
> God lost in the
> City of squares
> Out of a job and looking
> For his arm.

Thus lost, he looks "for believable/Joy to surface in the tame/
Eyes of all his own"—

> All who may mirror
> His lost way to the elevator
> Mad at the failed lights
>
> So they leave you alone
> It is all right
>
> All the windows (Look!) are now awake
> And yours, O Flowers![14]

There is here a rich spiritual experience into which the reader has
entered, making what he will of the "angry walks to the elevator,"
the "failed lights," and the windows that are "now awake" and
belong to the "Children" whom he calls "Flowers"—windows
that equate with light to illuminate their way who are Christ and
who in them has "lost his way." A poem of this nature must be
read as much more than a sum of symbol and allusion; it is a rich
spiritual experience.

Later and perhaps more strictly surrealistic poems are "The
Originators" and "A Carol," whose first drafts are found in the
early manuscript of *The Geography of Lograire,* both highly
corrected. In the former, one gathers that Merton's context is of
his personal influence on another through both his life and
writings. Because he chose "to hear a special thunder" in his
head, or sees "an occipital light," his choice suddenly "became
another's fate/He lost all his wheels/Or found himself flying."
But the influence turns out to be mutual, and when the other
caught in the "tame furies of a business gospel" (the first draft has
"the furies of some preacher's Bible"),

> His feeling was my explosion
> So I skidded off his stone head
> Blind as a bullet
> But found I was wearing his hat.
>
> Thus in art and innocence we fix each others fates
> We drink each other to gravestones.

But he warns:

> . . . my ideas
>
> Get scarlet fever evey morning
> At about four and influence goes out of my windows
> Over the suburbs
> Get out of the way of my ideas.
>
> I am wired to the genius you donated, the general demon.
>
> So one man's madness is another man's police
> With everybody's freedom we are all in jail
> O Brothers and Sisters here we go again
> Flip-flopping all over the circus
> With airs of invention.[15]

Another very personal and rather unusual poem, "A Carol," is also contained in the *Lograire* manuscript, though untitled and heavily corrected. It is addressed to "Juniors," as its first line indicates, which could refer to the young monks to whom Merton gave weekly conferences or, by extension, to anyone open to the advice in the poem's experience. (One might cite as its probable context the instance of back surgery which Merton had undergone in the spring of 1966.) The poem carries a refrain which changes incrementally as the poem proceeds. Images of fire and water are of its texture, with their attendant symbolism.

> When Jesus got my broken back for Christmas, Juniors,
> He learned what bloody parties seed from my sun
>
> He'd try my tissues with the simple question
> About the fire and water mixing in fun
>
> (O bloody water
> Never trust
> The military sun)

Then follow images cut loose it would seem from any poetic matrix:

> The chance of ages is a rock you'll jump from, Juniors,
> When Jesus has my waterwings and is alone out there
> Out in the sea where I must swim my Spanish
> Around the Puerto and the lucky phare.

For "waterwings" the uncorrected version has "bones," which may help in the metaphorical equating. Then the sudden conclusion, "And so I come to learn a new religion, Princess Mabel," cut off again from any previous referents; then water and fire meet images in the "skinny Baptist and my Catherine Cart-Wheel." And though legend states that St. Catherine was broken on the wheel, it may be that fire too had had its way. Then the Christmas reference, "see my borrowed body in the stable/Cutting one more cold night out of the funeral's domain/O Master of Timetables who will be the lucky one?" A final refrainlike stanza in the manner of a recapitulation closes the poem:

> When Jesus gets my broken back for Christmas
> And so many wizard babies of God are chosen
> To ride in a runaway train?
>
> (O bloody water
> Never trust
> The military rain).[16]

The poem's total impact carries with it in-depth insights on suffering and death—to the extent that the poet even desires death: "O Master of Timetables who will be the lucky one?" This poem might well serve as key to an enormous room of light—the poetry in which Merton excelled, as in the earlier "With the World in My Bloodstream," where he had named himself "a lost spark in Eckhart's Castle." Here the poetic experience goes far beyond the surrealistic juxtaposing of image and symbol; in the absence of any specific meaning, the reader must find his own, since the lines of the poem appear to be cut loose from the core of any dramatic context.

It seems well to close this study of Merton's late poems with the delightful and whimsical miniature drama, "Les Cinq Vièrges (Pour Jacques)," written for his friend, the late Jacques Maritain. The poem is based on the Gospel parable of the wise and foolish virgins invited to the "Marriage of the Lamb." The foolish ones ("hurluberlues") find themselves in a modern predicament, "Avec leur motos en panne/Et leur bibons de pétrole/Vides" ("With their motors out of order/And their gas tanks empty"). But, he says they had a saving grace, "Mais puisq'elles savaient/Danser/

On leur dit quand même/De rester" ("Since they knew/How to dance/They were told they/Might stay").

> Et voilà: il y avait
> Cinq vièrges hurluberlues
> Sans pétrole
> Mais bien engagées
> Dans le mouvement.
>
> Il y avait donc dix vièrges
> Au Noces de l'Agneau.[17]

And there they were, the five "vièrges hurluberlues"—"scatter-brained virgins/Without gas/But well involved/In the action." The conclusion: there were "dix vièrges/Au Noces de l'Agneau" —"ten virgins/At the Marriage of the Lamb." Typical Merton in a light, playful mood.

CHAPTER SIX

Recurrent Themes

There is no path to the summit—
No path drawn
To Grace's house.

After considering in some detail the several collections of poetry in the Thomas Merton canon (excepting the two last works published in his lifetime, *Cables to the Ace,* and *The Geography of Lograire*), it would seem pertinent at this point to cross chronological barriers in order to focus on poems dealing with specific subject matters that occur with a certain frequency.

It is unarguable that, whether overt or not, the ultimate referral point and matrix of all his writings—prose as well as poetry—is basically religious: the binding of man to God. Still, when considering the complete poetry canon, only about a third of the poems might be viewed as having specific religious themes. Among these a goodly number derive their inspiration from the Incarnation, with such events as proliferate from it—the Annunciation, Visitation, Nativity, Passion, and the Eucharist. In the first three the Virgin Mary's role is paramount, and since so many poems cluster around her, or are addressed to her, it seems important to isolate some of them for comment.

"The Blessed Virgin Compared to a Window" appears in Merton's first collection, *Thirty Poems* (1944), and at once conjures up Gerard Manley Hopkins's "The Blessed Virgin Compared to the Air We Breathe." Both poems elaborate a "metaphysical conceit": Merton's, the metaphor of a window representing the docile, pure soul of Mary through which God can transmit Himself unobstructedly as light through glass, and

Hopkins's, the trope comparing her to air surrounding and pervading us by her influence, since she has but "one work to do/Let all God's glory through."[1] Curiously, though Merton had read extensively in Hopkins, and while at Columbia had seriously considered writing a doctoral dissertation on his poetry, he never seems to have been influenced by Hopkins's sprung-rhythm prosody. It is also of interest to note that some ten years later, in a conference given the young monks at the abbey in his capacity of novice-master, Merton gave a careful analysis of the Hopkins poem.[2]

The metaphor of the window is not original with Merton nor with Hopkins. The latter speaks of "glass-blue days" and of "This blue heaven" (Mary) transmitting "The hued sunbeam [Christ] perfect, not altering it."[3] But the metaphor had earlier sources. While Merton was still at Columbia he became familiar with the sixteenth-century Spanish mystic, St. John of the Cross, and purchased a copy of *The Ascent of Mount Carmel,* which he read assiduously in his Greenwich Village apartment. The book is an extended commentary on a poem concerning the union of the human and divine wills, in which St. John used the comparison of a ray of sunlight striking a window.

> Although obviously the nature of the window is distinct from that of the sun's ray (even if the two seem identical), we can assert that the window is the ray of light of the sun by participation.[4]

But the metaphor was in turn borrowed by St. John of the Cross from the Pseudo Areopagite's *De Mystica Theologia* (Bk. II, Ch. 5).

Merton's poem begins:

> Because my will is simple as a window
> And knows no pride of original earth,
> It is my life to die, like glass, by light:
> Slain in the strong rays of the bridegroom sun.[5]

The word "simple" must be taken in its scholastic precisions, as having "no parts outside of parts" (St. Thomas). Merton uses it again in this same specific sense in a poem on St. Thomas Aquinas in which "the black-friar breaks the Truth, his Host,/ Among his friends the simple Substances."[6] The metaphor of the "bridegroom sun" is obviously from the Canticle of Canticles, a symbolism that appears frequently in spiritual theology. The poem continues:

> Because my love is simple as a window
> And knows no shame of original dust,
> I longed all night, (when I was visible) for dawn my death:
> When I would marry day, my Holy Spirit:
> And die by transsubstantiation into light.[7]

The reference to transsubstantiation and to the lover must again be given their full theological resonances.

Another Marian poem, and one of Merton's finest, is "The Messenger," a pre-Trappist poem first published in *Spirit,* then reprinted in *Thirty Poems,* and later in the poetry column of *The New York Times Book Review.* With Lady-day in its context of spring, the "annunciation imagery" is striking, as the "tongue of March's bugle" warns of "the coming of the warrior sun."

> When spring has garrisonned up her army of water,
> A million grasses leave their tents, and stand in rows
> To see their invincible brother.
> Mending the winter's ruins with their laughter,
> The flowers go out to their undestructive wars.

Then, counseling the flowers to "Walk in the woods and be witnesses,/You, the best of these poor children," Merton moves into the final stanza, which begins the swiftness of Gabriel's descent:

> When Gabriel hit the bright shore of the world,
> Yours were the eyes saw some
> Star-sandalled stranger walk like lightning down the air,
> The morning the Mother of God
> Loved and dreaded the message of the angel.[8]

In the poem "The Oracle," on a quite different theme, its final stanza alludes to Gabriel's swift movement of descent when

> . . . already, down the far, fast ladders of light
> The stern, astounding angel
> Starts with a truer message,
> Carrying a lily.[9]

And once again in "Aubade—The Annunciation":

> Desires glitter in her mind
> Like morning stars:
>
> Until her name is suddenly spoken
> Like a meteor falling.[10]

A related theme is that of the visitation of Mary to Elizabeth, on which Merton wrote two poems: "The Evening of the Visitation" and "The Quickening of St. John Baptist." In the former he asks nature to participate:

> Still bend your heads like kind and humble kings
> The way you did this golden morning when you saw
> God's Mother passing.[11]

Manuscript versions of "The Quickening of St. John Baptist" present an interesting study in development: the beginnings— two columns of pencil jottings (twenty-four lines) on a folded sheet, in which some of the key lines of the poem already appear, as for instance:

> Her salutation
> Sings in the stone valley like a Charterhouse bell.

Most of the poem is a questioning of St. John Baptist, and is couched in hermit imagery:

> . . . small anchorite!
> How did you see her in the eyeless dark?
> . . . . .
> You need no eloquence, wild bairn,
> Exulting in your hermitage,
> Your ecstasy is your apostolate,
> For whom to kick is *contemplata tradere.*

His vocation is with the Church's "hidden children":

> The speechless Trappist, or the grey, granite Carthusian,
> The quiet Carmelite, the barefoot Clare,
> Planted in the night of contemplation,
> Sealed in the dark and waiting to be born.

Night is our diocese and silence is our ministry
Poverty our charity and helplessness our tongue-tied
      sermon.
Beyond the scope of sight or sound we dwell upon the air
Seeking the world's gain in an unthinkable experience.[12]

In the second version of this poem (thirty-five lines), already the first line of the final version appears, "Why do you fly from the drowned shores of Galilee?" In the manuscript of the final version (seventy-one lines) the original title, "A Quickening: A Song for the Visitation," has been given its present title, "The Quickening of St. John Baptist," and dated Feast of St. John Baptist, 1947.

Another poem in the same collection, *The Tears of the Blind Lions*, "To the Immaculate Virgin, on a Winter Night," though written over twenty years ago, has a special contemporary significance, as Merton speaks of "a day of blood and many beatings"—

I see the governments rise up, behind the steel horizon,
And take their weapons and begin to kill.

There is also an allusion to the proximity of Fort Knox: "Out where the soldiers camp the guns begin to thump/And another winter time comes down/To seal your years in ice." The last lines of the poems are especially poignant:

Lady, the night has got us by the heart
And the whole world is tumbling down.
Words turn to ice in my dry throat
Praying for a land without prayer,

Walking to you on water all winter
In a year that wants more war.[13]

Another poem, the last with the Virgin Mary as theme, "The Annunciation," was written as a billet for the nuns of the New York Carmel and is in Merton's new manner, more free of elaboration, and in this instance somewhat reminiscent of a pre-Raphaelite painting:

The girl prays by the bare wall
Between the lamp and the chair.
(Framed with an angel in our galleries
She has a richer painted room, sometimes a crown.

> But seven pillars of obscurity
> Build her to Wisdom's house, and Ark, and Tower.
> She owns their manna in her jar.)
>
> Fifteen years old—
> The flowers printed on her dress
> Cease moving in the middle of her prayer
> When God, Who sends the messenger,
> Meets his messenger in her heart.
> Her answer, between breath and breath,
> Wrings from her innocence our Sacrament!
> In her white body God becomes our Bread.[14]

These poems form an easy transition to the theme of the Nativity, in which one is aware of the sensitivity, gentleness, and joy of their author's spirit in presence of this mystery, as in "The Holy Child's Song":

> When midnight occupied the porches of the Poet's reason
> Sweeter than any bird
> He heard the Holy Child.

In a type of envelope style, rarely used by Merton, the above three lines are used again as a refrain at the poem's end, enclosing the child's songs as they "Fly in and out the branches of my childish voice/Like thrushes in a tree."

> And when my Mother, pretty as a church,
> Takes me upon her lap, I laugh with love,
> Loving to live in her flesh, which is my house. . . .

In these poems nature is frequently used as setting—the winter season, and the animals, as the child continues his song:

> In winter when the birds put down their flutes
> And wind plays sharper than a fife upon the icy rain,
> I sit in this crib,
> And laugh like fire, and clap My golden hands:
> To view my friends the timid beasts—
> Their great brown flanks, muzzles and milky breath![15]

In the poem "Advent," in metaphor we find the animals again: "minds, meek as beasts,/Stay close at home in the sweet hay;/And intellects are quieter than the flocks that feed by starlight." The

moon and skies are invoked to "pour down your darkness and
your brightness over all our solemn valleys."[16] In "Carol":

> God's glory, now, is kindled gentler than low candlelight
> Under the rafters of a barn:
> Eternal Peace is sleeping in the hay,
> And Wisdom's born in secret in a straw-roofed stable.[17]

In "The Fall of Night," the farmers coming home from the
fields sing:

> We bring these heavy wagons full of hay to
> make your bed,
> O Mercy, born between the animals.[18]

Finally, in the poem "A Christmas Card," Merton paints a
winter canvas as

> . . . one by one the shepherds, with their snowy feet,
> Stamp and shake out their hats upon the stable dirt,
> And one by one kneel down to look upon their Life.[19]

Another frequent theme is that of children, to whom Merton
often alludes, especially in his early poems. It has been said that in
every poet there is a child, since in some fashion he invariably
retains a child's vision. Merton is no exception, and with this
vision has come an empathy with children that characterizes some
of his most sensitive poems. In "The Winter's Night," when "the
frost cracks on the window,"

> One says the moonlight grated like a skate
> Across the freezing winter.
> Another hears the starlight breaking like a knifeblade
> Upon the silent, steelbright pond. . . .
> Yet it is far from Christmas, when a star
> Sang in the pane, as brittle as their innocence. . . .
> The moonlight rings upon the ice as sudden as a footstep;
> Starlight clinks upon the dooryard stone, too like a latch,
> And the children are, again, awake,
> And all call out in whispers to their guardian angels.[20]

In "Aubade: Lake Erie," after the sun "light handed" has sown
"this Indian water/With a crop of cockles," Merton calls to the
children:

> Awake, in the frames of windows, innocent children,
> Loving the blue, sprayed leaves of childish life,
> Applaud the bearded corn, the bleeding grape,
> And cry:
> "Here is the hay-colored sun, our marvelous cousin,
> Walking in the barley."[21]

Again in "Evening" is the childrens' interpretation of nature:

> They say the sky is made of glass,
> They say the smiling moon's a bride.
> . . . .
> They name the new come planets
> With words that flower
> On little voices, light as stems of lilies.[22]

As Merton celebrated the candor and innocence of children, so too he was most vulnerable to their suffering. In an early poem, "Aubade: Harlem," "in the sterile jungles of waterpipes and ladders," he pictures a typical scene, one known to him firsthand, since before he entered the monastery he had spent many hours working in Harlem at Friendship House. The beginning and final stanza of the poem are the same, as we see.

> Across the cages of the keyless aviaries,
> The lines and wires, the gallows of the broken kites,
> Crucify, against the fearful light,
> The ragged dresses of the little children.[23]

One of the most interesting of Merton's poems on children is "Grace's House," written in 1962 and inspired by a four-year-old child's pencil drawing of a house on a hill.[24] With meticulous exactitude Merton details each object of the sketch—"No blade of grass is not counted,/No blade of grass forgotten on this hill." He details the house on the summit; a snow cloud rolling from the chimney; flowers; curtains, "Not for hiding, but for seeing out"; trees, from which animals peek out; a dog, "his foreleg curled, his eye like an aster"; a mailbox "full of Valentines for Grace".

> There is a name on the box, name of a family
> Not yet ready to be written in language.

In the second stanza appears the theme around which all resonances cluster, as Merton fastens on an apparently insignificant
detail which nonetheless provides the leitmotif of the poem,
namely:

> There is no path to the summit—
> No path drawn
> To Grace's house.

—which provides the contrast between our world and hers, "our
Coney Island," and her "green sun-hill",

> Between our world and hers
> Runs a sweet river
> (No, it is not the road
> It is the uncrossed crystal
> Water between our ignorance and her truth.)

The poem's last line re-introduces the theme, as Merton casually
mentions "a rabbit/And two birds"—

> . . . bathing in the stream
> which is no road, because

> Alas, there is no road to Grace's house![25]

Interestingly, the German edition of Merton's *Selected Poems* is
titled *Gracias Haus,* and the poem is first of the thirty-eight
which comprise the selection. On sending a copy of this edition to
a friend he remarked, "I think they did a very nice job. Glad my
little Grace made the title!"

At about the same time "Grace's House" was written, a newspaper photograph of a young Chinese refugee, stopped in her
flight to Hong Kong and kneeling in tears as she begged to be
admitted to the city, loosed in Merton a bitterly ironic poem, "A
Picture of Lee Ying," written in a free, almost documentary style,
as he mocks the platitudinal excuses offered by the authorities.

Point of no return is the caption, but this is meaningless she must
return that is the story

She would not weep if she had reached a point of no return what
she wants is not to return

Merton's irony cuts deep:

> When the authorities are alarmed what can you do
>
> You can return to China
>
> Their alarm is worse than your sorrow

But he tells her not to look at the dark side, for "You have the sympathy of millions." Then the devastatingly paradoxical conclusion:

> As a tribute to your sorrow we resolve to spend more money on nuclear weapons there is always a bright side[26]

Merton's mounting concern over the racial question found its expression in another children's poem, one of deep compassion, addressed to Carole Denise McNair, one of the children killed that tragic September of 1963 in Birmingham. The poem is titled "Picture of a Black Child with a White Doll" and is an implicit indictment of a society in which such a crime could happen.

> Your dark eyes will never need to understand
> Our sadness who see you
> Hold that plastic glass-eyed
> Merchandise as if our empty-headed race
> Worthless full of fury
> Twanging and drooling in the southern night
> With guns and phantoms
> Needed to know love.

This is in contrast to the irony that marked another poem, "And the Children of Birmingham," its sharp, objective, matter-of-fact statement set in the framework of a children's story, as it parodies "Little Red Riding Hood," "Grandma's pointed teeth/('Better to love you with')." The present poem, even as it contrasts the dark child with "That senseless platinum head/Of a hot city cupid," is pervaded by a tenderness that distinguishes its author:

> Next to your live and lovely shade
> Your smile and your person
> Yet that silly manufactured head
> Would soon kill you if it could think. . . .

So without a thought
Of death or fear
Of night
You glow full of dark red August
Risen and Christian
Africa purchased
For the one lovable Father alone.

And when all was done, "They found you and made you a winner"—

Even in most senseless cruelty
Your darkness and childhood
Became fortune yes became
Irreversible luck and halo.[27]

Not only to the suffering of children did Merton extend his concern but also to such as were caught up in some tragic circumstance or were victims of the judgment of an unhappy society. One of the most poignant poems Merton wrote, "There Has to Be a Jail for Ladies," is one in which he genuinely compassionates and pleads for the "ladies of the street," when "their beauty is taken from them, when their hearts are broken," while the government wants a jail for them "when they are ugly because they are wrong." He tells them:

I love you, unhappy ones. . . .
Tell me, darlings, can God be in Hell?
You may curse; but he makes your dry voice turn to
    butter. . . .
        He will laugh at judges.
He will laugh at the jail.
He will make me write this song.

And the last stanza carries an unforgettable image:

God will come to your window with skylarks
And pluck each year like a white rose.[28]

Like the seventeenth-century metaphysical poets whom Merton during his early student years much admired, he too wrote a number of elegies. The first, written for his brother, is well known and often quoted—"For My Brother: Reported Missing in

Action, 1943". A longer poem, "The Trappist Cemetery—Geth-semani," is addressed to his brother monks who lie in the burial ground circling the apse of the abbey church. Paradoxically, the poem is a song of joy rather than of mourning as Merton tells them not to fear that "The birds that bicker in the lonely belfry/ Will ever give away your legends," but exhorts them to look and "See, the kind universe/Wheeling in love above the abbey steeple/ Lights up your sleepy nursery with stars." In a somewhat effusive metaphor he recounts their lives, then asks that they teach us "how to wear/Silence, our humble armor. . . ./Because your work is not yet done," and at the last day, when "your graves, Gethsemani, give up their angels,"

> Return them to their souls to learn
> The songs and attitudes of glory.
> Then will creation rise again like gold
> Clean, from the furnace of your litanies:
> The beasts and trees shall share your resurrection,
> And a new world be born from these green tombs.[29]

This poem was recorded for the Harvard Vocarium Series by the British playwright Robert Speaight, and also included in the *Selected Poems* edited by him in England in 1950.

For "Elegy for the Monastery Barn," which first appeared in *The Strange Islands,* and later in Mark Van Doren's edition of Merton's *Selected Poems* (1959 and 1967), Merton furnished us the "poetic occasion," saying that it "was written after the cowbarn at Gethsemani burned down, one August evening in 1953, during the evening meditation. The monks left the meditation to fight a very hot fire and the poem arrived about the same time as the fire truck from the nearest town."[30] It received comment by Mark Van Doren in his introduction to *Selected Poems,* as he had requested to include this poem about which he knew Merton to be some-what shy. Merton remarked:

> As a matter of fact it is for me subjectively an important poem, because when I was a kid in Maryland (yes, even that, for a while) a barn burned down in the middle of the night and it is one of the earliest things I can remember. So burning barns are for me great mysteries that are important. They turn out to be the whole world, and it is the Last Judgement.[31]

In the poem the barn is presented under the image of an old lady who, for her last hour, had dressed herself in "Too gay a dress" and calls to the countryside, "Look, how fast I dress myself in fire!" But for those who worked in her she leaves vivid memories:

> She, in whose airless heart
> We burst our veins to fill her full of hay,
> Now stands apart.
> She will not have us near her. Terribly,
> Sweet Christ, how terribly her beauty burns us now!

But as legacy she has left them her solitude, her peace, her silence. Clustered around the metaphor of the barn is the monks' ignorance of her vanity, hence their surprise at seeing her "So loved, and so attended, and so feared." The "Fifty invisible cattle" return, and the past years as well "Assume their solemn places one by one" for this little minute of their destiny and meaning, as

> Laved in the flame as in a Sacrament
> The brilliant walls are holy
> In their first-last hour of joy.

The last two stanzas of the poem are reminiscent of the liturgy of Easter night relevant to the blessing of the new fire, Lumen Christi, which is later thrice plunged into the baptismal water. In both text and imagery the first line of the final stanza alludes to Luke 21:21, in which, foretelling the destruction of Jerusalem, Christ warns those in Judea to flee to the mountains and those in the city to depart.

> Flee from within the barn! Fly from the silence
> Of this creature sanctified by fire.

The second line touches on the petition "Sanctify this new fire," from the Exulet of the Easter night vigil. Merton continues:

> Let no man stay inside to look upon the Lord!
> Let no man wait within and see the Holy
> One sitting in the presence of disaster
> Thinking upon this barn His gentle doom![32]

Again there is an allusion to Luke (21:27), where "they will see the Son of Man coming in a cloud." The event of the barn fire is still kept in its spiritual dimension as it presents "the Holy/

One . . ./Thinking upon this barn His gentle doom!" It is *His* barn, since all things are His and He is all things, which recalls a moving passage in William J. Lynch's *Christ and Apollo,* speaking of the Christic imagination which

> begins to assume the order of creation and to lift it into its own vitality. Thus Christ is water, gold, butter, food, a harp, a dove, the day, a house, merchant, fig, gate, stone, book, wood, light, medicine, oil, bread, arrow, salt, turtle, risen sun, way, and many things besides.[33]

With its theological resonances and significances this elegy stands out among Merton's finest, as his poetic imagination lifts a simple event—the burning barn—through the zone of the Teilhardian cosmic Christ to that of apocalyptic vision.

Emblems of a Season of Fury contains four elegies. "Song for the Death of Averroës," is a simple narrative in verse-prose style, a form Merton was beginning to use in a number of poems, and is adapted from Ibn Al Arabi, after the Spanish version of Asin Palacios. The young man was sent by his father on an errand to his friend Averroës at the latter's request "to learn if it were true that God had spoken to [him] in solitude." Though at first troubled, Averroës afterward rejoiced and prasied God,

> . . . who has made us live in this time when there exists one of those endowed with mystical gifts, one able to unlock His door, and praised be He for granting me, in addition, the favor of seeing one such person with my own eyes.

Ibn Al Arabi never saw Averroës again, but attended his funeral in Cordova, and saw his coffin carried on one side of the beast of burden and the books he had written on the other. To a remark of the scholar Benchobair, "No need to point it out, my son, for it is clearly evident! Blessed be thy tongue that has spoken it!" Ibn Al Arabi set the words apart for meditation:

> I planted the seed within myself thus, in two verses:
>
> > "On one side the Master rides: on the other side,
> > his books.
> > Tell me: his desires, were they at last fulfilled?"[34]

In the same collection there are two occasional elegies, one for Ernest Hemingway, another for James Thurber. Merton speaks affectionately of Hemingway, who passes "briefly through our midst. Your books and writings have not been consulted. Our prayers are *pro defuncto N.*"

> How slowly this bell tolls in a monastery tower for a whole age, and for the quick death of an unready dynasty, and for that brave illusion: the adventurous self!

> For with one shot the whole hunt is ended![35]

That for James Thurber is written in a tighter structure as Merton entreats him.

> Leave us, good friend, Leave our awful celebration
> With pity and relief.
> You are not called to solemnize with us
> Our final madness.
>
> You have not been invited to hear
> The last words of everybody.[36]

Still another elegiac poem in the same collection, "An Elegy for Five Old Ladies," had its beginning in a *New York Times* report of their deaths, "ranging in age from 80 to 96," in a driverless car which, rolling across the lawn of a rest home, plunged into a lake.

> Let the perversity of a machine become our common
>   study, while I name loudly five loyal spouses of death![37]

One of Merton's late poems, "Elegy for Father Stephen," first published in *Commonweal,* is for a fellow monk, one of whose duties was to tend a flower garden and prepare bouquets for the altars of the abbey church. Merton calls him "Confessor of exotic roses/Martyr of unbelievable gardens"—

> Whom we will always remember
> As a tender-hearted careworn
> Generous unsteady cliff
> Lurching in the cloister
> Like a friendly freight train
> To some uncertain station.

The metaphors are strong fibered, yet the poem carries no sadness as Merton recalls chance meetings with the monk.

> Sometimes a little dangerous at corners
> Vainly trying to smuggle
> Some enormous and perfect bouquet
> To a side altar
> In the sleeves of your cowl.

But on the day of the burial,

> A big truck with lights
> Moved like a battle cruiser
> Toward the gate
> Past your abandoned garden. . . .

The closing lines of the elegy are tender and joyous:

> As if Leviathan
> Hot on the scent of some other blood
> Had passed you by
> And never saw you hiding among the flowers.[38]

Though at the time this poem was written, October 1966, Merton was already experimenting with surrealistic techniques, this elegy moves through clusters of simple yet strong imagery.

Another theme that runs through the fabric of much of Merton's poetry, if not explicitly then implicitly, is that of a denunciation of the so-called "world," though it is well to recall that in an entry in an early Journal, dated December 18, 1941, four days after his entering the monastery, he wrote: "I never hated less the world, scorned it less, or understood it better." Thus, he writes of the "city" because it is a symbol of much that dehumanizes man; even the titles of certain of his poems indicate this, such as the early "Hymn of Not Much Praise for New York City":

> . . . never let us look about us long enough to wonder
> Which of the rich men, shivering in the overheated office,
> And which of the poor men, sleeping face-down on
>   the *Daily Mirror*
> Are still alive, and which are dead.[39]

"In the Ruins of New York":

> This was a city
> That dressed herself in paper money.
> She lived four hundred years
> With nickels running in her veins.[40]

"And So Goodbye to Cities":

> For cities have grown old in war and fun.
> The sick idea runs riot.[41]

And in "How to Enter a Big City":

> Everywhere there is optimism without love
> And pessimism without understanding.[42]

The city as a symbol of "modern society" and the emptiness of technological man who, in conforming himself to its dictates, tends to lose all spiritual orientation was a frequent Merton theme. He had said of technology that it "alienates those who depend on it and live by it. It deadens their human qualities and their moral perceptiveness." Yet at the same time he realized that it was a fact and a necessity of modern life. Yet there is a danger—

> of technology becoming an end in itself and arrogating to itself all that is best and most vital in human effort: thus man comes to serve his machines instead of being served by them. This is completely irrational. One whom I have always admired as a great social critic—Charlie Chaplin—made this clear long ago in "Modern Times" and other films.[43]

In a poem, "First Lesson About Man," he ironically describes this condition:

> Man begins in zoology
> He is the saddest animal
>
> He drives a big red car
> Called anxiety
> He dreams at night
> Of riding all the elevators
> Lost in the halls
> He never finds the right door.

In brief, flat statements Merton continues his description: "Whenever he goes to the phone/To call joy/He gets the wrong num-

ber/He knows all guns. . . ./He flies his worries/All around
Venus. . . ./He drives a big white globe/Called death." The
"lesson" is logically followed by an interrogation:

> Now dear children you have learned
> The first lesson about man
> Answer your text
>
> "Man is the saddest animal
> He begins in zoology
> And gets lost
> In his own bad news."[44]

An earlier version of this last stanza read (two last lines): "And
that is where he generally/Ends."

But Merton's vision of what an ideal world, an ideal city should
be, he made explicit in his morality play, *The Tower of Babel*. As
set in Augustinian context, he contrasts the city of man with the
city of God—the former as symbol is destroyed "to give place to
the light which it might have contained."

> . . . This new city will not be the tower of sin, but the City of God.
> Not the wisdom of men shall build this city, nor their machines,
> not their power. But the great city shall be built without hands,
> without labor, without money and without plans. It will be a
> perfect city, built on eternal foundations, and it shall stand forever,
> because it is built by the thought and the silence and the wisdom
> and the power of God. But you, my brothers, and I are stones in the
> wall of this city. Let us run to find our places. Though we may run
> in the dark, our destiny is full of glory.[45]

CHAPTER SEVEN

Fugue Semiotique

But birds fly uncorrected across burnt lands
The surest home is pointless:
We learn by the cables of orioles

Already in *The Tears of the Blind Lions* and later in *The Strange Islands* Thomas Merton experimented in various poetic techniques with his use of image and symbol, irony and satire. However, it was in *Cables to the Ace: or, Familiar Liturgies of Misunderstanding,* that he utilized them in a viable working form in a species of antipoetry, which the book's blurb describes as an "animated mosaic of irony and experiment, parody and dour meditation." Of a first version sent to a friend in September 1966, Merton remarked, "I don't know what you will think of the book. I know many will be perplexed. Parts of it are O.K. I guess."[1] In a notebook of the same year he had written:

> The habit of anti-poetry is salutary. It opens up the riches of this sort of thing which a merely reasonable approach could not accept. It is not "practical." Cannot be used for monastic-renewal. But if you can't appreciate this there is no hope for renewal.[2]

This would seem to apply as well to readers of poetry.

This new literary manner is perhaps best described by him in an essay titled "Writing as Temperature," a review of Roland Barthes' *Writing Degree Zero* (1964). After speaking of *gestus* as the "chosen, living and responsible mode of presence of the writer in his world," he says:

> The authentic *gestus* of writing begins only when all meaningful postures have been abandoned, when all the obvious "signs" of

art have been set aside. At the present juncture, such writing can hardly be anything but anti-writing. The writer is driven back to the source of his writing since he can no longer trust the honesty of his customary dialogue with the rest of society.[3]

In so doing, Merton says, "he rediscovers something of the numinous power of the *gestus* which is charismatic only because it is completely modest." This necessitates a writing which is the exact contrary of "poetic" writing, as it rejects the "operable illusions" of the eighteenth- and nineteenth-century writers. Man must now come face to face with his own being, and that in a world of chaos. For this encounter he must possess a clarity of vision born of an inner solitude, a *sine qua non* of self-confrontation, for which, without doubt, Merton's writings on subjects of social concern—peace, race, the plight of the Indian—which antedate even his three years of hermitage, had amply prepared him.

As a consequence his world had marvelously expanded, and with this expansion had come a need for a new vehicle of expression that would offer the freedom to inject a complex multileveled meaning into his writing. For this purpose an "antipoetic" and surrealist technique seemed best suited. Thus, released from the bindings of traditional poetics, the new world of his imagination would be given the freedom it needed—a freedom that would enable him to successfully integrate the world of the irrational (or subconscious) with the rational to achieve not only unity and wholeness but a variety of scintillating effects. Awake to the possibilities of the subconscious, the dreamworld, he could later definitely state in the preface to his following work, *The Geography of Lograire*, that

> In this wide-angle mosaic of poems and dreams I have without scruple mixed what is my own experience with what is almost everybody else's.[4]

In the "Prologue" to *Cables to the Ace*, in a species of apology for what he foresaw would meet with questioning, he stated that he had "changed his address and his poetics are on vacation. He is not roaring in the old tunnel." And yet, "my ironies are no less usual than the bright pages of your favorite magazine."

In this long poem of eighty-eight sections, or entries, a unified blending of poetry, antipoetry, imaginative prose, and pointed quotation meet in an exciting collage in which at times Merton achieves a high lyricism, at others a devastating irony and black humor, as the subconscious spouts images without order or sequence that, in their however tenuous contiguity, result in a strange lucidity. André Breton, chief spokesman for surrealism, describes this perfectly when he says:

> It is, as it were, from the fortuitous juxtaposition of the two terms that a peculiar light has sprung, *the light of the image,* to which we are infinitely sensitive. The value of the image depends upon the beauty of the spark obtained; it is consequently, a function of the difference of potential between the two conductors. When the difference exists only slightly, as in a comparison, the spark is lacking.[5]

This quotation of Breton's has an added interest inasmuch as through the "cables," which are in themselves conductors, Merton makes an astonishingly frequent use of the electrical image, standing either in surrealistic positions or as symbols of our technological age:

> Some may say the electric world
> Is a suspicious village
> Or better a jungle where all the howls
> Are banal.
>
> NO! The electric jungle is a village
> Where howling is not suspicious:
> Without it we would be afraid
> That fear was usual.[6]

There are, moreover, "electric war," "electric eye," "electric sense," "electric world," "electric stars," "electronic renown," "psycho-electric jump," "electric palaces," "communions electriques," "electric lyres," "electrons," "electronic hospitals," and "electric promise." The figure is further extended in the use of "wires": "Found fifty persons all with wires in the pleasure center"; "They improve their imitable wire/To discover where speech/Is trying to go"; "Each ant has his appointed round/In the technical circuit"; "He enters the rusty thicket of wires"; and "Hanging on the wires." Thus Merton leaves no doubt as to the message-sending image of *Cables*. And at this point one is tempted to ask if he has not perhaps used to excess the nomenclature of the technological world, which he is obviously mocking. But that is precisely the force of the mockery.

A brief examination of the manuscripts of *Cables to the Ace* should be helpful in following the gist of the work and, to an extent, its final interpretation. Its nucleus and beginnings are contained in a small 8″ x 5″ ringed working notebook titled "Various 1965–1966," beneath which Merton had written, "Notes for Poems, Cables for an Ace, and Unpublished, August 1965." The notebook also contains various jottings and brief excerpts from his then current readings, such as Eliot's *The Sacred Wood*, Nietzche's *The Birth of Tragedy*, and, under the date of July 31, 1965, notes on Buddhism (Nikago). The first entries, which cover numerous pages, are in black ink; the mention of this is chronologically pertinent in dating entries, since Merton's method often entailed returning to pages of the notebook where spaces had been left empty and filling them in, sometimes with red, sometimes with blue ink. This method of interspersing entries in a layered fashion even physically conforms to Merton's plan to write a poem that is a mosaic.

Interestingly, the first entry in the notebook is that paragraph of poignant lyric prose which appears as No. 76 in the text, "After that we'll meet in some Kingdom they forgot. . . ."—which in the book follows in logical sequence from "I seek you in the hospital where you work. . . ." (No. 75 in the text). Too, the "Epilogue" of the work, beginning, "Now leaning over the salt nerve of our wave length. . . ." is one of a number of early entries and appears in the finished text with little or no revision. One suspects that the latter entry may at first have been intended as a prologue, since the present one appears neither in the notebook nor in the 1966 and 1967 manuscripts, and was likely entered in the final one together with the Zen-oriented entries. However, the holograph notebook presents a real "mosaic" of composition, with later entries fitted into the interstices between earlier ones. Here too is an occasional personal comment, such as a brief two lines slipped in between entries recalling a happy event of that day: "Everything! Piliated woodpecker, and everything!" There are also a number of comments on Bob Dylan, in whom Merton was particularly interested and on whom he was planning a study at the time of his death; for example, this emphatic judgment: "Bob Dylan is one of the most important voices in this country. . . . infinite variety." There are also a few bright lyric stanzas to the tune of "Frère Jacques," and a few phrases set to the melody of some Negro blues spiritual. But one of the most relevant to a study of Merton's poetry is that of an early entry in the same notebook in which he remarks:

> Well, it is poetry hour again. It is the moment of truth, the moment of effort. The unexpected word will suddenly be there with its new hat on. The unexpected sound wearing its dim little inarticulate fury and unable to be fitted in with the other children. But it is poetry hour and all must receive their due. Who knows but that the future will have to obey them.[7]

Too, there is a dream reverie, an exquisite descriptive piece, which one regrets Merton did not include in *Cables*. (He was known to have had vivid, interesting dreams.) This dream is in the manner of a prose poem:

> Came down by a sort of back stairway with a stone yard looking over the river, woods, cliffs. The then empty tourist buses parked in the yard. Woodsmoke comes in faintly out of the blue fresh valley. Postcards. Where? I have several times dreamed of this yard. Meeting the angel in that silent air. And down to the flashing waters. Will I go there again?[8]

Textually, *Cables to the Ace* presents an unusual structural arrangement. In September of 1966 a "first version" was completed and mimeographed, consisting of thirty-four selected entries, all of which are included in the expanded 1967 version (seventy-five entries), which later Merton was to further extend to eighty-eight entries and an "Epilogue." In the enlarged 1967 version some of the additional entries were copied out of the holograph notebook, others were of new material. Along with the first version, called at that time "Edifying Cables," Merton had planned to publish as Part II a collection of twenty-two new poems that had not yet appeared in any previous collection—the complete title of the work: *Edifying Cables and Other Poems*. The 1967 manuscript, however, dropped the poetry section, adding fifty-four new pieces to the then "Edifying Cables." The new, interpolated entries—some in holograph, some typewritten, and all heavily corrected and renumbered—together with pages taken over as they stood in the "first version," were inserted into the new manuscript. Most of the added pieces in the 1967 manuscript are newly composed, though a few are copied out of the original notebook.[9] So much for the book's architectural arrangement.

Apparently, when Merton decided to publish the manuscript of *Cables* as a unit without the originally planned Part II, he included in addition to the other entries the poem "Newscast" as No. 48, copied out of the holograph notebook, and "The Prospects of Nostradamus," No. 68, from the original collection marked Part II.

While working at *Cables to the Ace*, one of Merton's preoccupations and deep concerns was with language and linguistics. The quotation from Shakespeare's *The Tempest*, No. 6 in the book, was an entry added to the 1967 manuscript, when the work was practically complete, and appears in red ink in the upper margin of page 3 of the manuscript:

> You taught me language and my profit on't
> Is, I know how to curse. The red plague rid you
> For learning me your language! (Caliban)[10]

—which points to the fact that the Caliban image serves as a strand of the *Cables*, representing man at his most primitive. In connection with this there is an entry in the working notebook referring to Camus' *Sermon to the Seminarians*, and the quotation, "O go be Calibans in the salt city where the sun . . . hammers." Merton was at that time engaged in an in-depth study of Camus which resulted in four articles.[11]

But already in entry 3 of the 1966 manuscript Merton had stated:

Since language has become a medium in which we are totally immersed, there is no longer any need to say anything. The saying says itself all around us. No one need attend. Listening is obsolete. So is silence. Each word travels alone in a small blue capsule of indignation. (Some of the better informed have declared war on language.)[12]

The book's subtitle, "Familiar Liturgies of Misunderstanding," is also of special pertinence in this regard. The adjective first used was "home" liturgies (1966), then "heroic," and finally "familiar," which makes for sharp paradox, implying that a liturgy—a body of rites prescribed for public worship, and once familiar to the people—has now been rendered inexplicable, incoherent, incommunicable, and no longer capable of being interpreted. Throughout there are repeated references to the failure of communication: "We all have the same anxieties—but we do not use the same words. . . . Actually of course all the words are gendarmes and they stand around us in good condition."[13] And again, "return from the sudden sport to address/The monogag/The telefake/The base undertones of the confessional speaker."[14] And from the poem "Newscast":

> Printed joys are rapidly un-deciphered
> As from the final page remain
> No more than the perfumes
> And military shadows.[15]

These, then, are the cables strung to the "ace of freedom," in which context it is important to note that after discarding the first title, "Cables for the Ace," Merton named them, both in the 1966 and 1967 versions, "Edifying Cables." As Blake's achievement was "To see the world in a grain of sand," so too is Merton's miniscule of time and space pressed into a unit in which

> Your poem is played back to you
> From your own trump card
>
> Until all titles are taken away.[16]

The "Gem Notes" poem, an entry copied out from the working notebook for the 1967 manuscript, comes back on the cable as

> They improve their imitable wire
> To discover where speech
> Is trying to go.[17]

And in entry 16:

> Let choirs of educated men compose
> Their shaken elements and present academies of
>   electronic renown
> With better languages. . . .
> Let such choirs intone
> More deep insulted shades
> That mime the arts of diction
> Four-footed metaphors must then parade
> Firm resolution or superb command
> Of the luring innuendo.[18]

The poems and poetic prose that make up *Cables to the Ace* reverberate with allusions—literary, historical, musical, philosophic, theological—that only a writer of Merton's erudition could assemble. It might be a title, a phrase from some classic that is given an ironic twist—"O Comedy of Orders," "the ill-tempered clavicle," characters used humorously, or quotations upturned and trundled limpingly into the text—all serving to sharpen the impact of thought of the individual sections. For example, the Caliban quotation from *The Tempest*, beyond its pertinence to Merton's preoccupation with language and the failure of communication, presents as well a symbol of the earthy, the monstrous, the dehumanizing forces:

> Twelve smoky gates flame with mass-demonstrations.
> Power of Caliban. Mitres of blood and salt.[19]

And again:

> Future of transgression. It is in the homes of Caliban. A splendid
> confusion of cries. Politics of the inflexible mooncalf. A martial
> display of bulldozers. Dull energies in the dust of collapsing walls.
> Loose minds love the public muscles of death.[20]

And the unmistakable Prufrock echoes in the "tea phone" entry, with the Old Master (Eliot) who "worries about the code. [But] when he wakes he will have forgotten all his lines."[21]

Beyond the Shakespeare and Eliot echoes one might fill a page with allusions to various persons, places, and events: Blake, Plato, Descartes, even Santa in a delightfully funny satiric poem based on a quotation (author not stated) on "man's friendly competitor," the rat. Others are Finn, Bosch, Bernstein, Bach, Socrates, "Bonnie Braes," Angkor and Nîmes, Sartre and Ponge; St. Radegund, René Char, St. Anatole; and "Milton's friends—Republican, bituminous begin their scenarios in the dark stink of burning gasoline" (in the 1967 manuscript "Democratic" was crossed out and "Republican" substituted). To continue the listing: Batman, a hilarious take-off on *Newscast;* "the fevers of Vegas," Hopkins ("Leaden Echo," and "Come, Dark Haired Dawn"), Krushchev and Nixon ("Curtis is in the kitchen troubled with his enemies and all their mean sayings"), "Rape of the Sabines" at the Carnegie, the "priceless Flemings," Yeats ("I will get up and go to Marble Country"), Uncle Sam, Ursa Major, Texas oil, Joyce (Anna Livia Plurabelle), Houdini, Pocahontas, Jack's Capetown, Johannesberg, Rio, Caracas, Mexico, Fort Knox, Giant Mongrel (Caliban), Moscow, New York, China Sea, St. Joseph, "Catchmouse," Oliver Twist, Borealis, Vegetable King, Trojan War, Little Red Riding Hood, Funny Girl, Job's Queen, Giomar, Wordsworth, Coleridge, Thoreau, April stars, St. Theresa, Hunter, Capricorn, Bears, *Sanctus* sounds, Vox Humana, Prophets, the Muses, Taurus, E. E. Cummings ("dooms of love"), and Jack Sound—though this does not name them all. Truly, a revolving mirror of persons, places, literary works, and world events—all rotated through the lens of Merton's phenomenal imagination and focused on the world, the "electric jungle," and on the world of spirit. This antipoem of great complexity gives some insight into the multidimensional workings of Merton's mind, for it is alive not only with irony and satire but also with wit and humor, joined with that loving compassion so characteristic of its author.

As to the varied forms of the eighty-eight entries that constitute the work, there are a number of poetic genres used with more or less consistency. There are poems which despite their ironic content, such as "Weep, Weep little day" and "Prayer to Saint Anatole," still ring with the easy and graceful lyricism which we have learned to associate with Merton's early muse and his later poems of metaphysical tenor. A second type is the prose poem—descriptive paragraphs relating to his life as monk and hermit among the Kentucky knobs, "where the well-ordered hills go by, rank upon rank, in the sun." A third, the antipoem, is one of sheer ironic comment on the "electric jungle," image of a mechanical world.[22]

It was only in the final manuscript that Merton added the quotations from the Rhenish mystics Eckhart and Ruysbroeck and the Zen Master Dōgen, a poem on St. Theresa of Avila (from the *Cables* notebook), a poetic prose passage (in French) in the manner of René Char, with whose writing Merton was long familiar, and three entries, Nos. 37, 38, 84, which are his own personal comments set in the tonality of the Zen mystics, with entry 84 furnishing a key to the entire poem and to the identity of the "ace."

Though Shakespeare (Caliban, the primitive man) and Eliot (a "waste-land" in which Prufrock, the "mechanical" man is resident) are allusively an influence in Merton's *Cables*, they are only so as preliminaries to Merton's own voice as it takes over the poem's final summing up. Enriched as he was by his Zen mystical knowledge and experience, which made for a sense of unity, freedom, and a oneness with all reality, it would seem that at this point Merton decided to place the entire poem into final focus, thus bringing all strands together in a last centering: "The dove had flown into the fiery center of the vision."[23] And in entry 83 ("Solemn Music"), also from the notebook, Merton exhorts the reader:

> Take your compass
> To measure flight
> Expanding silences
> And pay attention
> To the stillness of the end
> Or the beginning.[24]

Already in entry 35, a series of poetic prose paragraphs in the manner of René Char, the succession of rare images created a mood which approximates the original vision—a state of quiet and peace:

> Je m'assieds dans mon champ vert comme un diamant tranquille.
> J'aborde le domaine bleu de l'air nu. Lumière et somme: la
> musique est une joie inventée par le silence.[25]

Then in entry 37 he speaks of the perfect act which only he who forgets "form" can see:

> Forget form, and it suddenly appears, ringed and reverberating with its own light, which is nothing. Well, then: stop seeking. Let it all happen. Let it come and go. What? Everything: i.e., nothing.[26]

Merton is already striving to articulate the "nothing" that is "everything," a state which only the true mystic has experienced.

> The way that is most yours is no way. For where are you? Unborn! Your way therefore is unborn.[27]

Entry 84 is quintessential Merton as, under title of *"Gelassenheit,"* he describes the "desert" and "void" in the spirit akin to Eckhart's "wilderness," wherein the true word of eternity is spoken. But the key to the full understanding of this complex, many-stranded poem's final focusing is in the following lines:

> But for each of us there is a point of nowhereness in the middle of movement, a point of nothingness in the midst of being: the incomparable point, not to be discovered by insight. If you seek it you do not find it. If you stop seeking, it is there. But you must not turn to it. Once you become aware of yourself as seeker, you are lost. But if you are content to be lost you will be found without knowing it, precisely because you are lost, for you are, at last, nowhere.[28]

This statement is strikingly analogous to the poem "The Fall" in *Emblems of a Season of Fury:*

> There is no where in you a paradise that is no place
>   and there
> You do not enter without a story.
>
> To enter there is to become unnameable. . . .
> Whoever is nowhere is nobody, and therefore cannot
>   exist except as unborn:
> No disguise will avail him anything
>
> Such a one is neither lost nor found.
>
> But he who has an address is lost.[29]

Entry 85, with its "flash of falling metals" and "shower of parts," a "Cataclysm of designs," was added, together with some eighteen other entries, after the 1967 manuscript was completed. Positioned as it is between entries 84 and 86—Merton's own Zen mystical description and the texts of Eckhart and Ruysbroeck—it points to an upheaval, inner as well as outer, that results in a "wilderness," where alone, as Eckhart states, "The true word of eternity is spoken," and where, according to Ruysbroeck, God's shadow enlightens "our inward wilderness." But "on the high mountains of the Promised Land there is no shadow." This leads logically to the "bell's summit" where, as Merton tells us, he is about to make his home.

He then moves swiftly toward the poem's apotheosis in entry 87, which first appears in the 1967 manuscript heavily corrected. As he nears the climax of his poem and its final definition he takes meticulous care with his word choices:

> I am about to make my home
> In the bell's summit
> Set my mind a thousand feet high
> On the ace of songs.[30]

This is actually the first time the "ace" has been mentioned, though it will occur again in the mystery of the poem's close, as mentioned in connection with the "summit." In *Zen and the Birds of Appetite* Merton writes that though Creator and creature are distinct,

> . . . [it] does not alter the fact that there is also a basic unity *within ourselves* at the summit of our being where we are "one with God."
> If we could identify purely with this summit we would be other than we experience ourselves to be, yet much more truly ourselves than we actually are. . . . it is only in this highest unity that we finally discover the dignity and importance even of our "earthly self" which does not exist apart from it, but in it and by it. The tragedy is that our consciousness is totally alienated from this inmost ground of our identity.[31]

Interestingly, the first line of the final stanza of entry 87, "I am about to build my nest," is used in the manner of a reprise of "I am about to make my home" of stanza one. Actually the latter was used as the first line of the final stanza, then changed to "take my rest," and only later to "build my nest," the former pointing directly to the "rest" of contemplation. The following line was changed slightly from "In the undirected express" to "misdirected and unpaid express." In the wording of the two final lines, "As I walk away from this poem/Hiding the ace of freedoms," there were also replacements. Merton's first choice was "poem"; he then changed it to "prophetic song," then back again to "poem." "Hiding the ace of freedoms" was first "In the ace of flights," then "In the ace of conquests," and finally, "Hiding the ace of freedoms." These alternative choices are significant in that they show Merton's careful search for the word or expression that would most exactly carry his thought in this climactic point of the entire work. The "ace of freedoms," though open to a number of approaches as to its meaning, in context of the late additions to the manuscript can point to nothing else but that state of soul in which "at the summit of our being" we are "one with God": the ace of freedom of spirit with its élan toward the contemplative life.

Merton's choice of "prophetic song," which he later changed back again to "poem," is equally apt and significant, inasmuch as today's religious orientation is toward a spiritual center of transcendent experience, as witnessed by the intensive study of Eastern religions, especially Zen Buddhism with its emphasis on contemplative awareness, and by the schools of transcendental meditation. Though the various charismatic movements serve as an overall witness to and search for God experience, the dynamism of their approaches differs widely.

Before leaving *Cables to the Ace,* certain of the lyrics, quite apart from their sequential patterning in the total work, invite comment, since they lend themselves to a number of interpretations. Entry 74 is one of them, as time shifts back to that of the early Romantic poets—Wordsworth and Coleridge—then merges with the present in similarities and contrasts. The poem appears flawless, perhaps the most perfect in the book, focusing directly on Merton the hermit in its first-line cry to God:

> O God do I have to be Wordsworth
> Striding on the Blue Fells
> With a lake for sale and Lucy
> Locked in the hole of my camera?[32]

Images form a personal parallel: "the Blue Fells"/the Kentucky hills; "the sorrows of animals/Which I keep in a pack on my shoulder"/a profound concern for humanity, in particular suffering humanity; "Walden Pond"/a possible reference to a lake on the abbey property (there are five); "football uniform"/the Trappist habit, which ties in with the lines, "Yet in my heart I knew he [the Vegetable King] had me/Figured for a minister." Then the Elias reference: "I am sustained/By ravens only and by the fancies/Of female benefactors" (the initial draft read "female poets")! In an assembling of these clusters of images and allusions one might point to a possible questioning of the hermit life, inasmuch as he faced urgings of certain friends who regretted his lack of opportunity to move about more freely and be more available to such as could profit by his presence—"Buy yourself an automobile!" The final, almost prophetic stanza of the entry would seem to bear this out, as he decides that it were

> Better to study the germinating waters of my wood
> And know this fever: or die in a distant country
> Having become a pure cone
> Or turn to my eastern abstinence
> With that old inscrutable love cry
> And describe a perfect circle.[33]

Actually, the first line and a half of the stanza could be taken literally (there was a spring near the hermitage whose waters made Merton ill), but the line could well extend to a fever of spirit to turn to the East (which was now an "abstinence"). Too, "the germinating waters of my wood" could metaphorically define his in-depth study of Zen, which was knowing a progressive development. The dying in a distant country is frighteningly prophetic, especially when read in context of three lines in entry 34:

> Oh the blue electric palaces of polar night
> Where the radiograms of hymnody
> Get lost in the fan![34]

The "distant country," the "Eastern abstinence," the inscrutable "love cry," ("OM"), and the "perfect circle" seem mysteriously to predict his death in Bangkok on December 10, 1968, exactly twenty-seven years from the day he entered the monastery. However, though stanzas two and three state possible alternatives resulting from his inner questioning, his final answer is to remain. This already appears in the 1966 manuscript; he had made his decision.

Another outstanding lyric is entry 80, in which for the first time in the work Christ is named. He appears coming slowly "through the garden/Speaking to the sacred trees," as Merton evokes the setting and atmosphere of Christ in Gethsemani. He finds his lost disciple not only sleeping, but "hiding":

> Slowly, slowly
> Christ rises on the cornfields
> It is only the harvest moon
> The disciple
> Turns over in his sleep
> And murmurs:
> "My regret!"[35]

An early poem, "The Regret" (*Thirty Poems*), set in an autumn landscape, carries much the same spiritual ambience:

> Acorns lie over the earth, no less neglected
> Than our unrecognizable regret:
> And here we stand as senseless as the oaks,
> And dumb as elms.[36]

But in the former poem, the disciple *will* awaken and understand "When he knows history." Meantime:

> . . . slowly slowly
> The Lord of History
> Weeps into the fire.[37]

It is precisely here, as Merton comes to the close of *Cables* where the various strands meet in the "ace," that Christ is presented seeking the disciple, whose consciousness when he awakens will find itself transformed into the consciousness of Christ, the "Lord of History."

Entry 45, a lyric exquisite in verbal music, is "Prayer to Saint Anatole":

> Anatole, Anatole the long jets
> String their hungry harps
> Across the storm
> When everybody cries
> In the chemical flame.

Anatole was a third-century bishop of Laodicea, who during the siege of Brachium at Alexandria aided the poor and suffering. The "Long jets," the "chemical flame," the "Fivestar Generals," and "Riot and War" point up the present conflict, made more specific in the last stanza:

> Anatole Anatole
> The fairy bombers
> The fatal recorders
> The electric lyres.[38]

Coincidentally, in the notebook of *Cables* there is a single stanza of a poem titled "Prayer to St. Ambrose," in the same verbal rhythms, of which the Anatole poem seems to be something of an echo, and may well have been its original form. It begins:

> Ambrose, Ambrose
> The fearful harps
> Are playing at the fire
> And where the fire-lords are
> Riot and war. . . .[39]

Later, Merton likely decided that St. Anatole was more pertinent to the subject of contemporary war "When everybody cries/In the chemical flame."

In the *Virginia Quarterly Review*, a reviewer of *Cables to the Ace* (no name given) sums up his comments by stating that "It is essentially a book of love poetry." True. This message to the age, an ironic and witty variously structured antipoem, rich in allusion and aimed at a technological society that dehumanizes man, can have had its genesis only in a heart permeated with God's love and love for all humankind. As the reviewer concludes, "For all the irony, parody, and wit of this interesting volume, it is poetry rich with affirmative possibility."[40]

Present as well in this work are poignant overtones of the love of friendship, a human dimension which need not be passed over because of Merton's monastic dedication. As an artist, and an extremely sensitive human being graced with rich depths of spirit, Merton had a capacity for love and friendship given to few, together with its special genius for sharing. As a young monk he had been much attracted to the English Cistercian, Aelred of Rievaulx, whose treatise on friendship (with its roots in Cicero's *De Amicitia*) was to him a source of intensive study. In September of 1968, a short three months before his death, he had completed an article on "The Monastic Theology of St. Aelred" as preface to a book by A. Hallier, in which he says:

> The natural basis for this theology of friendship is of course the indestructible inclination to love, which is the divine image in us. . . .[41]

—a love, which variously endangered, can be healed and re-directed only in Christ. In an interview in *Motive,* and in the beautiful prose poem "Day of a Stranger," he remarks specifi-cally on this theme. So one need not be surprised that in cables strung to the ace there are overtones nuanced by human love. Given the gift to go out to others in love—and it *is* a gift—it follows that its renunciations are especially keen. Yet its entire tonality is ultimately affirmative. We find lines in entry 12 such as "Another sunny birthday. I am tormented by poetry and loss. . . . My loneliness is nourished by the smell of freshly cut grass, and the distant complaint of a freight train. . . ./All the symbols have to be moved." And again, "What have the signs promised on the lonely hill? Word and work have their measure, and so does pain. Look in your own life and see if you find it." There are entries that are even more explicit; especially touching is the final stanza of the poem "The Harmonies of Excess," a new entry added to the 1967 manuscript:

> For the lovers in the sleeping nerve
> Are the hope and the address
> Where I send you this burning garden
> My talkative morning-glory
> My climbing germ of poems.[42]

Love is joy, and in the dimension of renunciation love is pain, but not a loss, rather a gain, whose sheer poignance matures and enriches the human spirit. So real was this theme to Merton, and so great his empathy for others, that even into a poem of ironic thrust he could weave it with deep sensitivity and skill.

CHAPTER EIGHT

World of Myth and Dream

I am one same burned Indian
Purple of my rivers is the same shed blood
All is flooded
All is my Vietnam charred

Thomas Merton in the Author's Note to *The Geography of Lograire* speaks of its being "only a beginning of patterns, the first opening up of the dream." This pattern and dream, though a self-contained unit, he considered but the "first part of a work in progress," as he remarked to his publisher when submitting the manuscript in the summer of 1968 before his departure for Asia and his tragic death in Bangkok.

At about the time Merton was thinking along the lines of a poem of this kind, he mentioned in one of his notebooks that he would like to do something in the manner of a collage, a mosaic, in which thought standing against thought, and mirroring each other kaleidoscopically, would result in a synthesis from which a total meaning would emerge. His concern was with wholes, interactions, infrastructure. It was to this that he set himself in beginning *The Geography of Lograire*, a mosaic of immense proportions, encompassing as it does his own simple yet enormously complex world—a world that was not his alone but everybody's, though it be posited in the geography of the poet's thought and articulated in his own select symbols and images. It was as well a personal search for his own "self-location."

The name of the imaginative country of his poem, "Lograire," is Merton's own creation—a name derived from the family name of the French lyric poet François Villon (des Loges), with its relevances to the hut or cabin where, as a hermit, Merton spent the last three years of his life. By extension it applies as well to all the places in the world where he or anyone else has lived, and since, in a sense, each man has his own imaginative "Lograire," how does he or anyone else locate himself in the geography of all men?

Merton divides his world into four parts, which is everyman's universe, a map labeled "South," "North," "East," and "West" whereon he contrapuntally charts his own personal journey against theirs, using re-imagined historical and anthropological texts that he weaves into a tapestry of myth. Among these texts are African legends, Mayan religions, trials of the Ranters of seventeenth-century England, Kane's Relief Expedition, the Cargo Cults of Melanesia, the Ghost Dances of the American Indians, and numerous others—a veritable potpourri of rich historical and legendary material whose facts become in Merton's dream and poetic invention a species of myth. Each division of the poem has its own specific structural orchestration proceeding by contrast as do the movements of a symphony.

It is well known that Merton kept an astonishing number of working notebooks with excerpts from his readings, first drafts of poems, and occasional personal comment in the manner of a diary—a habit which to a writer with Merton's peculiar genius was quite "native." It is said that on one occasion Merton remarked that he could not think without a pen in his hand. As was the case with *Cables to the Ace,* so too with *The Geography of Lograire,* he kept a copious working notebook which contains the greater part of the manuscript of the book, though in a somewhat different arrangement. The manuscript is of prime interest since it contains some of Merton's latest writing, including a few poems and fragments of poems, notes from readings, and manuscript worksheets. Titled "The Newsnatch Invention," the forty-seven-cent notebook from the Rutgers University Bookstore has its cover marked in two places with "Fr. Louis" (Merton's name in religion)—made with a stamp designed by one of his novices, who cut out the letters on both sides of an eraser—and is signed: "By Thomas Merton, 1967." It is possible that "The Newsnatch Invention" may have been the original title of the proposed work. After the second stamp of his name is an epigraph from Gaston Bachelard: *"Rendre Imprévisible la parole n'est-il pas un apprentissage de la liberté?"*[1]

Merton's use of the term "invention" harks back to the logic of classical rhetoric, wherein each piece of writing began with "invention," the choosing or devising of a subject, followed by "arrangement," then "style," which throughout Merton's work is as flexible and individual as his gift might dictate and as recognizable as his handwriting. Some of the first entries in the notebook are especially interesting. Under title of "the new," one can imagine Merton's many notebook beginnings re-lived, as its first entry, in the manner of reminiscence, self-examination, and decision, begins with short sentences:

> And the New. Beginning Easter. Forty-seven cent notebook.
> Don't go back any more. Finished with keeping. Stirring up
> explanations. No more.
> You are tied to the old by the same words.
> A word: "Freedom" is also a prison.
> Do not want to say "I know."
> Instructions, Assumptions.
> Pretending to know. To be one of the knowers.[2]

Then his mind goes back to an early love, St. John of the Cross, now known in light of a mature knowledge, as he questions:

> If I would now go to Spain and *see* those stones for instance at
> Segovia
> And *see* those spaces (Castilla la-viega).
> Drink some of that wine feel some of that sun, some of that wind
> It's true raw bit in the spring
> And there read John of the Cross over again
> All in Spanish . . . Or would the same old wheel keep turning?[3]

Then follow fragments of poems, completed poems heavily reworked, and various notations, among the latter "participles/By which to tread water," water-treading a figure familiar to Merton and clarified in a short personal poem that follows the notation:

> A Sunday afternoon
> All the rosebuds in flower
> Nobody home.

> I walk in bare feet
> Learning the ground
> Dry cut trails
> The true needles of pine
> And a thistle near
> Where I turn.
> To tread water
> To believe—to tread water)[4]

Another poem, "Plutarch: of a Barbarian," echoes Blake; then follow five short lines in the tone of an exorcism:

> O all my Junes!
> Out of the cabin (cribbed confined)
> O let my Junes
> (Old Pharaoh)
> Out of the cabin![5]

Then a jotting, by way of a first motif for the poem, "Carol": "When Jesus met my hormones in the straw crib he reproved nothing./Juniors, learn!" followed by a much re-worked first draft of the poem, with incidental rhyme and an incremental refrain, both unusual with Merton. A heavily corrected first draft of his poem "The Originators" follows, and "Lubran," lightly corrected. There is a curious piece—five holograph pages in poetic form—which deals with cybernetics and the computer. About the latter Merton was deeply concerned, and his preoccupation with the number "10" seems eerily prophetic of the date of Merton's death: December 10, 1968.

> It didn't often both 10, 10, 10, eyes
> Including station well 8, 2, 4, oh
> Tracy get hold of the bubble 2, 2, 2,
> It surfaces in 9, 9, 9, power
> Don't you all agree?

This goes on solemnly for five pages, seeming to focus on the same mysterious note as it plays around the number "10." Further snatches of lines read:

> Mean 10, mean 10, mean 1, mean 1,
> . . . . says 10
> Says 10, says 10, says 10 system of the barter system
> . . . .
> This is track 10, 10, 10
> Gol says log Cybern will make 10 megacycles
> . . . .
> Ut us Omega you mega 10 death you mega
> O you mega
> Mega pay the debt for all his tumble not fun.

Then startlingly:

> So morior morior and is 2 time gone to his Principl . . .
> Gone to the kindly Principl in cybernetica mori
> Meum at 10 propositum decem
> To die my death in the cybern . . .[6]

So far the poems and fragments of poems—of which there are several more—in the manuscript preceding the opening Prologue. The title of the work does not appear until page 35 of the manuscript, beneath a quotation from Chateaubriand:

> Chaque homme porte en lui un monde composé de tout ce-qu'il a vu et aime et ou il rentre sans cesse alors même qu'il parcourt et semble habiter un monde étrange.
>
> (Chateaubriand)[7]

Only a portion of the printed "Prologue: The Endless Description" (sixty-nine of its one hundred seven) is here and used with very slight editing though in a different arrangement. It presents motifs introducing an autobiographical element as Merton reconstructs the landscape of Wales in a surrealistic manner, now more perfected than in earlier writing, together with his genius for evoking "the spirit of place": "Green tar sea stronghold is Wales my grand/Dark my Wales land father it was green." As if at random, in a blend of sea imagery and literary and biblical allusion, Merton unscrolls his ancestral background:

> 5. Plain plan is Anglia so must angel father mother Wales
> Battle ground opposites in my blood fight hills

Plain marshes mountains and fight
Two seas in myself Irish and German
Celt blood washes in twin seagreen people[8]

Shifting to Cambridge we find him "A Welshist player on the rugged green at Clare" (his college), then back to the New Forest and Beaulieu wood:

Minster in the New Wood Minster Frater in the grassy
Summer sun I lie me down in woods amid the
Stone borders of bards.[9]

In *The Seven Storey Mountain* he mentions this afternoon "lying in the grass in front of the old Cistercian abbey."[10] Then back to "Wales all my Wales a ship of green fires":

Gone old stone home on Brecon hill or Tenby harbor
Where was Grandmother with Welsh Birds
My family ancestor the Lieutenant in the hated navy
From the square deck cursed
Pale eyed Albion without stop.[11]

Merton's paternal grandmother, Gertrude Grierson, died at the age of one hundred two in New Zealand, where the family had gone in 1856. Merton's great-grandfather's name was James (so too was Merton's middle name): "Wash ocean crim cram crimson sea's/Son Jim's son standing on the frigate."[12] Though Merton's grandmother's father was Scotch, her mother was Welsh, hence the family name Bird. In a relevant passage in *Conjectures of a Guilty Bystander*, Merton writes of the Birds, and especially of his grandmother, of whom he retained the strongest impression:

But the best that is in us seems to come from her Welsh mother, whose family name was Bird. This is where our faces come from . . . the look, the grin, the brow. It is the Welsh in me that counts: that is what does the strange things, and writes the books, and drives me into the woods. Thank God for the Welsh in me, and for all those Birds, those Celts, including the one who was a lieutenant in the navy, and whose face, in a miniature which Aunt Maude had, is said to prove all this. Aunt Maude, too, had the Birds' face, and the humor, and the silences.[13]

The Prologue establishes the personal element of the work—Merton's ancestral world—as a prelude to the world he will create in the landscape of *Lograire*. In a sense they are one, as he proceeds to find himself in the geography of all men.

One of the pertinent elements in *The Geography of Lograire* is Merton's use of parody. This literary device he manipulates with great skill to point up some of the characteristics of a sterile culture, notably the falsity of its advertising, the confusion of politics, and the exploiting of its technology. Yet despite the caustic criticism implicit in his parody, its tone remains gentle, urbane, and saturate with humor.

One of the most striking examples of his use of this technique occurs in Part IX of the "South" canto, where, using as his referent Miguel Covarrubias' *Indian Art of Mexico and Central America*, descriptive of their pottery, resembling Picasso's, their food, women's clothing, hairbleaching, and other cosmetic customs, Merton takes occasion to parody modern advertisements, such as those in *The New Yorker:* "A most provocative perfume/ Wicked charms/Natural spray dispenser/A special extract/For four-eyed ladies of fashion/MY SIN . . ." In Part I of the "North" canto, "Queen's Tunnel," which is largely autobiographical of Merton's early years in New York and England, there is a veritable network of parody. Consonant with the neosurrealistic narrative in which Merton's "wakeful dreaming" expresses itself, are parodic lines such as "The time has come for Auld Lang Syne to forget and for the business to part companies," and again, "My prayers are all torn out of the mourning paper."

In Part I of the "West" canto is the poem "Day Six O'Hare Telephane," descriptive of sights and sounds at an international airport where "Big Mafia sits with mainlining blonde/Regular Bounder Marlo/Come meet the world muffin at ticket counter," and later of the plane in flight where "Sinbad returning from Arab voices/With his own best news for everybody boy/Says: 'Wellfed cities/Are all below/Standing in line/Beneath enormous gas/Waiting to catch our baseball.'" And in Part II of the same canto, in the poem "At This Precise Moment of History," which Merton situates at "About the time Shirley Temple/Sat on Roosevelt's knee," he records the "Voice of little sexy ventriloquist mignonne: 'Well I think all of us are agreed and sincerely I myself believe that honest people on both sides have got it all on tape. Governor Reagan thinks that nuclear wampums are a last resort that ought not to be resorted.'"

In his parodies Merton's message is clear, and whether it be spoken subtly or blatantly, it is always with humor and highly effective in underscoring his critical concern for the betterment of contemporary society.

In "South", Part I of the work, are eleven individual sections—poetry and prose—of a varied nature, among them a grouping of eighteen prose paragraphs, again with autobiographical overtones—"I am the way to Louisville in the end."[14] The remaining sections are based on Merton's readings in a range of cultures, including an African lament, a Hottentot parable, a passage in W. C. Willoughby's *The Soul of the Bantu*, a Mayan festival honoring the god Ce Xochitl, and *The Book of Chilam Balaam*. One of the most intriguing is "The Ladies of Tlatilco," from the Ce Xochitl festival as discussed in *Indian Art of Mexico and Central America* by Miguel Covarrubias, with illustrations of animal-shaped artifacts which Merton describes:

> 1. Effigy vessels shapes of apes
> Men peccaries rabbits coons ducks acrobats and fish
> Long charming little bottlenecks pots bowls
> And inventions:
>> For example
> "when liquid was poured out of the funnel-shaped tail
> The animal's ears whistled softly
> In a double gurgling note."
>> (Covarrubias)[15]

Merton proceeds by way of direct quotation from the book, followed by descriptions in personal arrangement interspersed with gentle satiric comment based on contemporary advertisements from *The New Yorker*:

> 8. A most provocative perfume
> Wicked wicked charms
> Natural spray dispenser
> A special extract
> For four-eyed ladies of fashion
> MY SIN. . . .

12. Two ways to tell a primitive bath figurine
With an expensive look
Your skin can tell
"All her goings graces"
In taupe or navy
Cashmere lovat wine
In maize my moons
O so serene
In cardigan charcoal blue
Shetlands hunter green.[16]

"Notes for a New Liturgy", originally published in *Poetry*, is a humorously ironic description of certain aberrations in a "dreamed liturgy" wherein "a big Zulu runs our congregation/A woe doctor cherubim chaser/Puts his finger on the chief witch . . ./ Knows all the meanings at once/Knows he is in heaven in rectangles/Of invented saints." A fantastic dream poem with, one suspects, hints of a clerical critique: "I dreamt this Church I dreamt/Seven precious mitres over my head/My word is final."[17]

Of "North," the first part of the second division of the work, Merton remarks that it is the most personally subjective, and specifies "the long meditation on Eros and Thanatos, centering in the New York City Borough of Queens," a dream that in diffuse focus reaches out to London and other places in Europe. It returns to focus sharply on the gasometers of Elmhurst, and other places on Long Island, where the "Top funnel house" was, in Merton's words, a presence "structured into society" and symbolizes death. In this waking-dream sequence one can recognize places and events of Merton's student years in New York (1938–39) while attending Columbia University, all arranged in an undefined and nebulous running commentary with a Joycean multileveled meaning.

Since at this time he resided with his mother's relatives in Douglaston, Long Island, these are the places he knew well:

3. Most holy incense burners of Elmhurst save us. Most Coronas
screen us. House of Hungarians feed us. Give us our Schenley labels
from day to day. Give us our public lessons of love. Swimming
grunt lights down to the bottom. Even the Island is long won.
Trams to the end. House of Hungarians spare us. Holy incense
burners of Elmhurst dissolve us. Trains come and gone.[18]

It is interesting to note that this portion of *The Geography of Lograire* is copied from the holograph manuscript with scarcely any correction, though in the printed text there are several additions and interpolations, also a vulgarity or two that are absent in the original. If the notebook pages are a first draft, as they undoubtedly are, it is apparent they were written with little interruption, almost in the manner of automatic writing, so spontaneous, free, and fluid are the lines. "A surrealistic meditation," as Merton remarks in the Prologue.

All the walls have high grey teeth and tickle the night with signs.
All the nights are children of chicken movies. We came home early
only to write back to the same movies: "wishing you were here!"
The city of verticles. The verses of comicals. The time has come for
Auld Lang Syne to forget and for the business to part companies.[19]

The poem which serves as a Prologue to the "North" canto, particularly "Queens Tunnel," is a quiet lyric, "Why I Have a Wet Footprint on Top of my Mind." It sets the stage for the first section, as the poet walks along "Around the formerly known/ Places/Like going/When going is knowing/(Forgetting)." Then, meditatively:

> To have passed there
> Walked without a word
> To have felt
> All my old grounds
> Forgotten world
> All along
> Dream places
> Words in my feet. . . .
> *Geography*
> *I am all (here)*
> *There!*[20]

Time past is now, so too place, as the kaleidoscopic world of Merton's unconscious unfolds panoramically in the very personal "Queens Tunnel," variously allusive as it names scenes of his early life merging with personages of Anglo-Saxon history.

29. North is LNER wending off Scotch Nero's in the dark.
Aberdeen pudding and cobbles. Scotch fisheries. Lake kipperies.

The Loch Mess Mumps. The Nordsee haggis. Cuthbert is on his
rock warmed by the noses of seals. Hilda on the Hilltower, Bede at
his desk, Caedmon in the pub, and Grace sings all her loudest
alarms for Old King Cole.[21]

Absurdities and truths continue to alternate to the final prose
stanzas:

49. Dear Togs. I have chosen electric life with spades. The lines
here are almost new. Home is underwater now. Conscience is a
bronco well busted. Memory secured by electronic tape. Gunshots
on the glassy swamps of night. Uniforms wade under willows
calling to the dead.

50. So Christ went down to stay with them Niggers, and took his
place with them at table. He said to them, "It is very simple much
simpler than you imagine." They replied, "You have become a
white man and it is not so simple at all."[22]

Part II of this canto is a lyric poem based on a quotation from
Blake's *Jerusalem*, II, 41, 15: " 'There is a grain of sand in Lambeth
which Satan cannot find.'/There is a child of God in the sacred
cellar. . . ." Merton recalls the time preceding his father's death
in London. He is staying in Ealing, at his Aunt Maude's, and his
father, though ill, is still with them. The manuscript lists a final
stanza which has been omitted in the printed version:

> The child's father will lie confused in the next room
> His eyes already troubled with death
> And the boy will know nothing
> Only the sins that fill him with a worse trouble
> The silent presence of the lamps of the Watch. . . .[23]

—for, as he writes toward the end of the poem, "a child must die
into manhood/On the cricket field":

> There is a grain of sand in Lambeth which Satan
>   cannot find
> While deep in the heart's question a shameless light
> Returns no answer.[24]

Parts III and IV of "North" are adapted from Merton's readings: "The Ranters and Their Pleads" based on the documents

and trial of certain members of a seventeenth-century fanatical sect, and "Kane Relief Expedition" (1855), on descriptions in the Journal of Dr. James Law, in the Stefansson Collection at Dartmouth. In the latter, one of the finest pieces in the book, are beautiful descriptive passages—poetry alternating with brief sections of prose—as Merton, condensing and editing the text, makes his own arrangement:

> Morning came at last
> The storm over we sighted
> Quiet mountains green and
> Silver Edens
> Empty country—Near?
> (We were deceived—30 miles at least)
> . . .
> "One iceberg on our port bow
> Resembled a lady dressed in white
> Before her shine"
> (Dazzling whiteness
>   gemm'd with blue-green)
> "In the attitude of prayer"
> . . .
> We climbed to a graveyard
> High on the wet rock
> There bodies sleep in crevices
> Covered with light earth then stones
> Some were sailors from England
> And America
> Now asleep
> In this black tower
> Over Baffin's Bay
> Waiting, waiting
> In endless winter.
> We left them to their sleep
> Ran down to meet the living girls
> . . .
> We called for a Polka. The band
> "Struck up Camptown Races we had taught them
> The previous night"
> Seizing our partners
> We all commenced

Better dancing
I never saw at home.

. . .

"Light streaming through a tall archway in a berg
Like scenes in the showy fairy pieces
At the theaters."[25]

The "East" of Merton's geography, "LOVE OF THE SUL-
TAN!" is in ten sections, each based on his readings, beginning
with "East with Ibn Battuta," then "East with Malinowski,"
followed by "Cargo Songs," seven selections relating to a cult in
which Merton had a deep interest and about which he had taped a
long lecture-essay titled "Cargo Theology." In a letter to Naomi
Burton Stone, as given in the notes to the text, he explained that
the Cargo movements originated in New Guinea and Melanesia
toward the end of the nineteenth century, though there were
analogous movements elsewhere, especially in former colonial
countries. He described them as messianic or apocalyptic, con-
fronting a crisis of cultural change

> by certain magic and religious ways of acting out what seems to be
> the situation and trying to get with it, controlling the course of
> change in one's own favor (group) or in the line of some inter-
> pretation of how things ought to be.[26]

In a certain sense Merton considered Marxism a species of
Cargo cult. Though much of the cults' belief may appear absurd,
Merton, together with certain anthropologists, have found in
them a deep meaning which could apply universally, since the
belief springs from an unshakable faith in fundamental human
worth. This the cults demonstrate. These "Cargo Songs," with
bibliography, might well have made a book in themselves. In
them Merton uses his usual technique of alternating direct documentary quotation with personal editing and poetic arrangement, in some instances short unrhymed lines with occasional
insertions of prose, in others the narrative prose paragraph. An
example from "Sewende (Seven Day)":

1. Seven Day in an unknown country where aspirins
   come from

And pants and axes and corned beef in cans
It is beyond the green sea, the white sea, the blue sea
Past Tokyo North America and Germany
But in the same direction
Far far beyond other countries
No one has seen this blessed land.[27]

Again, from the "Cargo Catechism":

7. Jesus Christ is now in Sydney waiting to deliver Cargo to natives
without the intervention of white men. He has a steamer and it is
all loaded. But he does not yet have the proper clothing. Jesus
Christ is waiting in a hotel room for someone to bring him a suit.[28]

In Part X, "And a Few More Cargo Songs" is based on *From a
South Seas Diary* by Peter Worsley. John the Broom is introduced:

> . . . a big man with shining buttons
> He is hidden from women
> (Except Gladys a little girl)
> He will provide the money
> . . .
> 5. Ghost wind come O Brother
> Sell me the shivering
> For a little piece of paper
> Sell me the shivering
> For a little piece of Whiteman Times
> To roll my cigarette
> To blow my Whiteman smoke
> In Ghostwind good feeling
> O sell me the shivering brother
> Give me a ticket to the happy dark
> Trade me a houseful of rifles
> For a new white skin
> In Dark Ghost Wind
> Sell me the shivering, Brother,
> For Whiteman good times![29]

But perhaps the most intriguing piece in the book is "Day Six
O'Hare Telephane," which introduces "West." The locale and
jargon of traffic at an airport, and on a plane in flight, depict a
trip to San Francisco. Merton made such a flight in May of 1968
en route to the Cistercian monastery in the Redwoods. From

Louisville there was a plane change at O'Hare Field in Chicago, hence the poem's title. Interspersed with the description of flight runs a counterpoint of seven brief texts from the *Ashtavakra Gita* (translated by Hari Prasad Shastri) addressed to the subconscious mind of a contemplative as his senses play on the hurly-burly of sights and sounds at the airport and during a cross-country flight.

Realism and surrealism mingle in Merton's portrayal of pre-flight traffic at the airport:

> Comes a big slow fish with tailfins erect in light smog
> And one other leaves earth
> Go trains of insect machines
> Thirty-nine generals signal eight
> Contact barrier four

> A United leaves earth
> Square silver bug moves into shade under the wing building . . .
> Please come to the counter
> Where we have your camera
> Eastern Airlines has your camera
> And two others drink coffee
> Out of yellow paper cups.

> Big Salvador not cooled off yet
> From sky silver but
> Hotel Fenway takes off at once
> To become Charles' Wain.

Then the first Hindu text:

"The wise man who has acquired mental vacuity is not concerned with contemplation or its absence."

Again, in landscape of the airport:

> Big Panam leaves earth . . .
> Small dapper North Central is green for woods
> And arrives safe
> Flight information requires Queen
> All green Braniff leaves earth for Pole
> And big United Doppelganger slides very close
> Seeking the armed savers

Then as if in a race "Over the suburban highschools/Our glide has won"—

> We leave earth and act
> Going to San
> Patterns slide down we go for clear . . .
> San Franciscan wing over abstract
> Whorls wide sandpits watershapes
> Form and prints and grids
>
> Invent a name for a town
> Any town
> "Sewage Town."
> And day six is a climbing sun
> A day of memory.

Between images of flight is another Hindu text addressed to the traveler: "Having finally recognized that the Self is Brahman and that existence and non-existence are imagined, what should such a one, free of desires, know, say or do?"

> Should he look out of the windows
> Seeking Self-Town?
> Should the dance of Shivashapes
> All over flooded prairies
> Make hosts of (soon) Christ-Wheat
> Self-bread which could also be
> Squares of Buddha-Rice
> Or Square Maize about these pyramids
> Same green
> Same brown, same square
> Same is the Ziggurat of everywhere
> I am the one same burned Indian
> Purple of my rivers is the same shed blood
> All is flooded
> All is my Vietnam charred
> Charred by my co-stars
> The flying generals.

The unity of man in his universe—his desires, upliftings, sufferings. Then the text: "He who sees reality in the universe may try to negate it." But not so he who sees it as *one*.

Merton names the flight "a day of memory," and so skillfully does the poem proceed that one has the sense of flying with the poet over

> . . . the porcelain edges
> of the giant Mother Mississippi . . .
> Dubuque dragging its handkerchiefs
> Into a lake of cirrus.

The descriptions of airscape and landscape together with that of personalities aboard the plane, some but lightly disguised, make for an intriguing portrayal: "Sinbad returning from the vines of wire/Makes his savage muffled voice/With playboy accents/ To entertain the momentary mignonnes/As if he meant it all in fun"; big Mafia who "sits with mainlining blonde"; and "Regular Bounder Marlo," called "to meet world muffin at ticket counter." The poem concludes:

> *Merveilles!* Secrets! Deadly plans for distant places!
> And all the high males are flying far west
> In an unanimous supermarket of beliefs
> Seeking one only motto
> For "L'imagination heureuse":
> WHY NOT TRY EVERYTHING?[30]

Surely one of the most original and exciting poems, as the ordinary events of a simple cross-country flight filter through the creative mind of a poet versatile as Merton.

Though "Day Six O'Hare Telephane" does not appear in the manuscript of *The Geography of Lograire,* the poem that follows it in the text, "At This Precise Moment of History," does, with its politico-satiric overtones laced with humor:

> 1. At this precise moment of history
> With Goody-two-shoes running for Congress
> We are testing supersonic engines
> To keep God safe in the cherry tree.
> When I said so in this space last Thursday
> I meant what I said: power struggles.

In sixteen different stanza patterns in which real or veiled names are used, the poem continues: "Dr. H.," earlier referred to as "Hanfstaengel," who left in disgust "About the time Shirley

Temple/Sat on Roosevelt's knee." And in stanza eleven we hear
the voice of "little sexy ventriloquist mignonne":

> "Well, I think all of us are agreed and sincerely I myself believe that
> honest people on both sides have got it all on tape. Governor
> Reagan thinks that nuclear wampums are a last resort that ought
> not to be resorted." (But little mignonne went right to the point
> with: "We have a commitment to fulfill and we better do it
> quickly." No dupe she!)[31]

In the printed version of this poem two final paragraphs are
omitted from the manuscript version; there is also an inter-
changing of lines, names added, and names omitted, and interesting word changes. For example, "nuclear wampums" instead
of "nuclear weapons," and Governor Reagan's name has been
added to the printed text, though not appearing in the manuscript. Merton was a careful writer, but one can imagine him,
tongue in cheek, spinning out the satire and gentle irony of this
unusual piece.

The subject matter of the two final parts of "West," the concluding canto of The Geography of Lograire, lies in the area of
Merton's social concern for the plight of the American Indian.
Both "Ghost Dance: Prologue" and "Ghost Dance" (which the
notes indicate are chronologically reversed in the text) are drawn
from historical documents on a series of interwoven religious
cults deriving from Indian prophecies and superstitions. These
originated about 1869 among the Paviotso Indians near Walker
Lake in Nevada and shortly thereafter spread to other tribes
of the western United States. The first, "Ghost Dance: Prologue,"
is based on a government document and the statement of "American Horse," a leader who clarifies his grievance:

> We were made promises by the Comissioners but we never heard
> from them since.
> They talked nice to us and after we signed they took our land cut
> down our rations.
> They made us believe we would get full sacks if we signed but
> instead our sacks are empty. . . .
> We are told that if we do as white men do we will be better off but
> we are getting worse every year.[32]

Merton's method is that of condensation and selection, as he introduces characters as they appear in the original documents. In "Ghost Dance," based on prophecies, we find:

6. Zonchen reported that he had seen the dead coming. They were on their way. I saw Zonchen when he was down in Reno fifty years ago. I don't know whether he was just a chief or whether he dreamed these things himself.

7. The Starter said the dead were on their way with the Supreme Ruler. They were all coming in a group. No distinction would exist any more between races.

. . .

19. Dr. George came to the mouth of Lost River where he found Captain Jack and the people. He came in winter when no grass was growing. He said that when the grass was eight inches high the dead would return. The deer and all the animals would return. "The whites will burn up and vanish without leaving any ashes. Dance or you will be turned to stone."[33]

And so the American Indian takes his place with Africans, Hindus, Stone Age men, and a multitude of others in the all-encompassing panorama of Merton's imaginative world of *Lograire.*

At the close of the "Author's Note" to this remarkable book, Merton states that the poems constituting the work "are never explicitly theological or even metaphysical." Still, given their author, in his "wide-angle mosaic of poems and dreams" it is inevitable that they be at least implicitly so. Further, given their subject matter, the universal struggle of love and death in a world that is both Merton's and ours, they are bound to spell out an eschatology, since he is dealing with the experience of Everyman.

As to the form of this extraordinary work, Merton names its tactic that of an "urbane structuralism," concerning which an unsympathetic reviewer remarked that in our critical point in history we can well do without "puzzle poetry." But is this "puzzle poetry"? Is immediacy of communication the pivotal element in poetry? Is not the *logical* meaning of a poem only one of the elements of the complete *poetic* meaning? *Le style c'est l'homme,* wrote Buffon, and given a man as complex as Merton—even his close friends concede this—it was entirely in keeping with the quality of his mind that as he came to a more all-encompassing worldview, the form of his writing was bound to adapt itself to his expanded vision. For form finds itself in content and is inextricably linked to it. Hence, should fragmentary phrasing, syntax in verbal turmoil, and surrealistic structuring best approximate his thought, Merton did not hesitate to use them. His tactic was not so much a *tour de force,* much less an exercise in deliberate obscurity, but a necessity born of the very nature of his vision. And though at times diverse and random, the poem's underlying logical structure results in an exceptional unity.

CHAPTER NINE

The Poet's Crystal

Should the dance of Shivashapes
All over flooded prairies
Make hosts of (soon) Christ-Wheat
Self-bread which could also be
Squares of Buddha-Rice

Merton has been dead many years. On first thought it would seem presumptuous even to begin an attempt at an evaluation of his voluminous writing, much less the very quintessence of the artist's craft, his poetry. But in face of the impressive corpus of the latter—six collections, two extended poetic works, and well over fifty late poems only recently entered in a collection—one might at least make a start.

For the poet the creative act is one of deep complexity. In an early essay, "Poetry and Contemplation"—first published in *Figures for an Apocalypse,* later revised and reprinted in the 1959 edition of *Selected Poems*—while electing for the primacy of contemplation, Merton drew analogies between the two, inasmuch as poetry reaches out by intuition into areas of knowledge that transcend the material, while contemplation intuits the very ground of being, God within.[1] And it would seem true to say that any critic in evaluating Merton's poetry would necessarily have to take into account not only his monastic commitment, but in that commitment, and paradoxically as it might seem, born of it, his continually expanding thought.

The manuscript collection of poems from which Merton made his first selection for *Thirty Poems* (1944) and a portion of those in *A Man in the Divided Sea* (1946) is the same, the residue having been published posthumously as *Early Poems* (1971) twenty-five years later. Many of these poems, especially those which deal with classical themes, exhibit a technical brilliance combined with colorful imagery along taut surfaces, as even then Merton was familiarizing himself with techniques sufficiently flexible to lend themselves to whatever form his content might demand. But it was not until his third collection, *Figures for an Apocalypse,* that his poems became almost exclusively "monastic" both in their motifs and their settings, vibrant with the color and line of the Kentucky landscape immediately surrounding the abbey. It was then that the poetic tensions discernible in the earlier poems were relaxed and replaced by the long, loosened line. Merton, on a graph which he drew up for a studies course on his writing, rated this collection "Poor,"[2] though in presenting external nature as an epiphany of being the book is a compelling example.

Already in his *Early Poems* Merton was preoccupied with certain social issues which in his later work ranged widely from racial and other injustices to the tragedy of war. "Dirge for the World Joyce Died In" illustrates this with its plea to "Rescue the usurers from the living sea."[3] And in "Two British Airmen (Buried with ceremony in the Teutoburg Forest)," he calls on the bugle to "Supersede the Parson's voice/Who values at too cheap a rate/These men as servants of their state."[4] At this time the integrity of the poet also concerned him, as in "The Strife Between the Poet and Ambition," where the poet is robbed by money and fame, "who broke the cages and let go/My aviary of metric birds,/And all the diction in my zoo/Was let out by the amateurs!"[5]

In Merton's fourth collection, *The Tears of the Blind Lions* (1949), one notices the beginning of a breakthrough in technique by his introducing the individual "I" into a number of poems. There is also a greater verbal density and in a few poems a certain starkness of statement which in his later writing would serve him well as a vehicle for the expression of his overriding theme—the mystical experience. And while the poems in *The Strange Islands* (1957) show an ever-increasing social involvement—as witness the verse-drama, *The Tower of Babel*—the techniques of individual poems tend to tighten and lean toward the simple and unadorned line. But most important, it is here that Merton begins to give glimpses of the contemplative vision which in his next collection would become more overt. In *Emblems of a Season of Fury* (1963), in addition to a number of poems which deal with what one might call a Zen mystical dimension, the "inner experience," are also poems of ironic comment on conditions subversive to man's freedom—whether based on an event of recent history, such as the much reprinted "Chant to be Used in Procession Around a Site with Furnaces," or on a current newspaper photograph of a Chinese refugee, as in "Picture of Lee Ying."

In Merton's later poems, now gathered in his *Collected Poems* (1977), his technique can be seen to have been progressively changing, as he begins to experiment with surrealistic structures, exemplified in "A Round and a Hope for Smithgirls," "Sensation Time at the Home," and "A Tune for Festive Dances in the Nineteen Sixties." His themes too are more existentially oriented, as in "With the World in My Blood Stream," where he speaks openly of his deepening personal involvement.

In a word, as the world moved into situations of greater complexity, Merton moved with it, not only in theme but also in manner. He was ready to experiment with concrete poetry,[6] and if such fragmentary jottings as "Kandy Express" entered in a notebook on his Eastern trip are any indication, he was well on his way to evolving a descriptive poetry of vivid immediacy.[7]

In Merton's first extended poem, *Cables to the Ace* (1968), consisting of eighty-eight discrete entries of poetry and poetic prose, his contemporary relevance is the more specified. His myth of concern is expressed in ironic vision, parody, and antipoetry that sound a comic as well as a tragic note in a veritable fugue of the absurd. On the book's back cover Merton comments that "At first sight it may look subversive but it can safely be given as a Twelfth Night present, without the slightest fear of damage to anyone, even to Catholics."[8] Throughout the entries his critical thrusts are directed at a technological regime that fails to communicate to man as total man but solely to him as mere robot to do its bidding. Flowing from this state of things Merton recognized such factors as loneliness, meaninglessness, and alienation, the latter resulting "When culture divides me against myself, puts a mask on me, gives me a role I may or may not want to play."[9] However disparate the strands in this kaleidoscopically woven work, they are finally gathered together and strung to the "ace of freedom"—the Godhead as *Urgrund*, infinite, uncircumscribed freedom.

In a beautiful lyric, No. 74 in *Cables to the Ace*, Merton refers to his "eastern abstinence," this inner urge to open himself more deeply to the contemplative East. But as he continued to gaze into the many-faceted crystal of his imaginative world, he saw with increasing clarity that his world and the élan of his spirit were everybody else's as well, whether they be sustained by the "Christ-Wheat," "Squares of Buddha-Rice," or "Square Maize about those pyramids," as he states in his last work,

> *The Geography of Lograire:*
>
> Same is the Ziggurat of everywhere
> I am one same burned Indian
> Purple of my rivers is the same shed blood
> All is flooded
> All is my Vietnam charred.[10]

This truth was graphically brought home to us after Merton's tragic death, when his casket was brought back to the States in an American army jet beside the caskets of his "Vietnam charred" brothers.

In this long, last work of Thomas Merton, *The Geography of Lograire*, part of a larger projected work, yet a contained unit in itself, he mixes the personal with the universal in the experiences of men of various times, finding that however bizarre their beliefs and superstitions may seem to us, they are not too unlike our own. Here is Merton at the peak of his powers, not sparring for the truth of some abstract philosophical or theological thesis, but with incisive insight, wit, and compassion, seeking to probe the diverse experiences of existential man. And one can but conjecture what basic profundities he might have reached had he been able to complete this last work.

Since today Merton stands alone as a contemporary poet of any considerable stature who was a monk, it is logical to expect he will be dealing with religious themes, or if writing on mundane subjects, that their overall focus will be religious. One might note here that there is a certain sense in which any poet can be considered a religious poet, since under the outer appearances of things he discerns their spiritual innerness. Each poet has his individual vision which closes in on the *mythos* in which he works. Merton's central vision was the Christian context in which man's ultimate calling is to contemplation. This it was that shaped and controlled his performance as a poet. Contemplation, he said, is not a "thing" which "happens"; he had previously been much concerned with its being interfered with by the poet's aesthetic intuition. "In actual fact," he said, it belongs "to the mystery of what one 'is,' or rather 'who' one is."[11] And he said further that "poetry 'is' contemplation," inasmuch as the poet sees beneath surfaces to the mystery within. Since both these intuitions involve man's total being, far from interfering with each other, there should be a mutual heightening and intensification of the one by the other.

From the testimony of Merton's writings and from those who knew him intimately, it is safe to assume that he had experience of both conatural knowledges—aesthetic and contemplative—which placed him in a privileged position to speak authentically of each. For him the poet's intuition, his awareness of reality as modified by a seascape, a flower, a religious ritual, a loved person, reaches out to grasp the latent perfection of things. Any object pointing beyond itself to an "other" speaks of that "other" whether anyone knows it or not. This is the burden of one of his most significant poems, "Song for Nobody," in which "A yellow flower/(Light and spirit)/Sings by itself/For nobody. . . ./Let no one touch this gentle sun/In whose dark eyes/Someone is awake."[12] For Merton, as for Hopkins, this uttering of itself of the individual object subsumes all mystery, whose unknowableness, while so remaining, is nevertheless articulated in image and symbol.

Perhaps it is in place at this point to refer to the distinction which Merton made between authentic religious poetry and mere "devotional verse." Indeed, he had long posited analogues between the aesthetic and mystical experiences. In *Bread in the Wilderness* (1953), speaking of the Psalms as the simplest and greatest of all religious poems, he explains that the experience which they carry is not only poetic by religious standards, which he sharply distinguishes from "devotional verse," but springs from a true religious (not necessarily a mystical) experience.

Devotional poetry is verse which manipulates religious themes and which does so, perhaps, even on a truly poetic level. But the experiential content of the poems is at best poetic only. Sometimes it is not even that. Much of what passes for "religious" verse is simply the rearrangement of well known devotional formulas, without any personal poetic assimilation at all.[13]

He further compares devotional verse to a game of "poetic checkers" which makes use of a number of devotional clichés, adding that a truly religious poem is not born of a mere religious purpose. "Art that is simply 'willed' is not art."

Before attempting a final word on the Merton poetic *oeuvre* it would seem unfair to him not only as a poet but as a human being not to mention a native exuberance and merriment of spirit which characterized him as witness to the freedom of the children of God, "everybody making joy," as he once remarked. Even a chance meeting would convince one of this delight of spirit, and despite the grave tone of the majority of his poems, he had a light and playful touch as well. While still a young monk he wrote a series of humorous limericks for a member of the Trappist community who had undergone serious surgery at a Louisville hospital. Frequently in the working notebooks one comes upon snatches of witty verse that would subtly shade into the semiserious. One such is "Antipoem I," a poem addressed to a moth, beginning: "O the gentle fool/He fell in love/With the electric light/Do you not know, fool,/That love is dynamite?"

> Keep to what is yours
> Do not interfere
> With the established law
>
> See the dizzy victims of romance
> Unhappy moths!
> Please observe
> Their ill-wandered troth.
>
> All the authorities
> In silence anywhere
> Swear you only love your mind
> If you marry a hot wire.

Obstinate fool
What a future we face
If, one and all
Follow your theology

You owe the human race
An abject apology.[14]

There is humor and wit as well in Merton's concrete poetry. A first impetus in this technique may have come from his study of the Chinese ideogram when working at a translation of the poetry of Chuang Tzu. We come upon his first ventures in the genre in the final issue of *Monks Pond* (No. 4, 1968), where he superimposes on a photograph of a Kentucky distillery the word "whiske," which he proceeds to shape in a perpendicular column of nineteen variations in letter and word. Equally interesting in the same issue is "Semiotic Poem from Racine's 'Ephigénie,'" arranging the text "ces morts/cette lesbos/ces cendres, cette flamme" in four different patternings.

In *Collected Poems* we find a selection of twelve concrete poems including the two mentioned above, three of them constructed of a simple word or phrase, as "Hurluburlu," "Ovid," and "awful music." But one of the most intriguing is "Found Macaronic Antipoem," which Merton explains in a footnote was taken from an Elementary Reader, Augsburg, 1514, and consists of six alternate lines in Latin and in their German translation. To this Merton adds his own off-beat rendering, which he places upside down on the page, beneath the original. For example, the Reader's "Stateram ne transgrediaria" set above its German translation, "Zau nicht uber die schmir./Obermachs nit./Trit nicht über das syl," becomes in Merton's rendering: "Don't mess with the scales/ Don't slice over the line/Nix overmake/Don't drive through the back/Of the garage." Merton's exercises in concrete poetry are not only strikingly original, but his careful concern with the physical shapes of letter, words, and phrases in his design present a pleasing visual image, which is what concrete poetry is all about. In the working notebook of *The Geography of Lograire*, between more serious entries, we find an airy little verse for a Christmas card, with its final pun line:

O good snow bell some wonder were you well
Fare thee well o fair I will not wonder well
I know no where well I know snow where
I Noël.

It is a sheer joy to witness the verbal resiliency of a serious poet who can turn his gift to delightful play—an entirely logical proceeding; for with a fine sense of the balance of things as referent, he can easily recognize the imbalance, which serves as excellent theme for light verse.

In résumé, Merton's poetic progress appears to have moved gradually, then swiftly in a cyclic diffusion from the controlling center of his spiritual élan to its apogee, culminating in poetry of contemplative vision. This comprised not only the "inner experience" of the mystic but, in a pure awareness, the direct intuition of the ground of being which subsumes all metaphysical as well as mystical experience.

In a "Message for Poets," sent to a group meeting in Mexico City in February of 1964, he had written:

Let us be proud of the words which are given to us for nothing, not to teach anyone, not to prove anyone absurd, but to point beyond all objects into the silence where nothing can be said.[15]

This was Merton's central vision—the God-awareness at the center of one's being. And this was his essential theme, whether implicit in the earlier poems, or explicit—though veiled in metaphor—in the later ones. Nor does this mean to understress the areas of his social concern which in his later works were to become so widely inclusive. For these sprang from this contemplative center as their matrix—a continuum of experience that was world-encompassing as sieved through the creative mind of a man whose spiritual horizons were limitless.

Merton then, was well in the tradition of such religious poets as St. John of the Cross, Donne, Hopkins, Auden, and Eliot. But in his cosmic vision and contemporaneity he stands in a special relevance to our day. His contemplative vision was anything but exclusive. And the hermitage of the last three years anything but an enclave—rather, it was one "of a thousand windows" through which "he watched our world (loving it) and chose it/his ash-

ram.''[16] And it was from this contemplative center within himself that he reached out to the East, where for lama, rimpoche, bhikku, and sufi, contemplative awareness constitutes a way of life. His emphasis on the "inner experience" has a special relevance to today's world with its frantic reaching out for various forms of self-transcendence. In a letter to Aldous Huxley (November 27, 1958), in reply to his article in *The Saturday Evening Post* on drugs as help in achieving the experience of self-transcendence, Merton closed by saying:

> May I add that I am interested in Yoga and above all in Zen, which I find to be the finest example of a technique leading to the highest *natural* perfection of man's contemplative liberty. You may argue that use of a koan to dispose one to Satori is no different from the use of a drug. I would like to submit that there is all the difference in the world, and perhaps we can speak more of this later.[17]

Merton's journey to Asia in September of 1968, specifically to address a group of monastic leaders in Bangkok and an interfaith group in Calcutta, was for him personally to learn and test for himself, to share and be shared, and hopefully, to find in the life of contemplation a *point de départ* for the meeting of East and West.

In sum, Merton's uniqueness as a religious poet lies in his focusing on the "inner experience," as he called it, the God-encounter in the depths of one's being and his striving to articulate it in his poetry. That this essential theme has its relevance for contemporary man in his seeking for transcendent experience is beyond dispute. And all of this Merton could validly contain within the scope of his monastic commitment. Though he may have seemed daring at the start—and there remain those who still question his final direction—one might conclude by way of comparison with another religious poet, Hopkins, who like Teilhard de Chardin inscaped Christ at the heart of all creation. So too Merton's distinctive voice sounds at the *point vièrge* of the human spirit in its God-encounter. This is the leitmotif of all his poetry, whether expressed in the delicate Zen mystical lyric in which he excelled or in the barbed ironic thrusts of his antipoetry, as in that stunning mosaic, *Cables to the Ace.*

A panoramic study of Merton's poetry might well be closed by the final lines of a poignant memorial written by his poet-friend Daniel Berrigan, titled "Funeral Oration for Thomas Merton as Spoken by the Compassionate Buddha":

> The monk Merton I take up in lotus hands
> To place him in the eternal thought
> A jewel upon my forehead.[18]

NOTES

CHAPTER ONE

1 "Tom's Book," diary kept by Thomas Merton's mother, Ruth Merton, during the first two years of his life.

2 Besmilr Brigham, "day is yellow; ce xochitl (dept to Nahuatl)," *Monks Pond*, No. 2. (Summer 1968), Trappist, Kentucky, pp. 3-4.

3 Thomas Merton, "Answers for H. Lavin Cerda," *Punto Final* (August 1967), Chile, p. 1.

4 Thomas Merton, *The Seven Storey Mountain* (New York, 1948), p. 409.

5 Ibid., p. 410.

6 Ibid., p. 236.

7 Ibid.

8 Thomas Merton, "Hymn of Not Much Praise for New York City" (manuscript); *The Collected Poems of Thomas Merton*, p. 19 (hereafter cited as *Collected Poems*).

9 "Dirge for the World Joyce Died In" (manuscript); *Collected Poems*, p. 3.

10 Thomas Merton, *Cables to the Ace* (New York, 1968), p. 24; *Collected Poems*, p. 418.

11 "La Comparsa en Oriente (A Conga)" (manuscript); *Collected Poems*, p. 9.

12 *Thirty Poems* (New York, 1944), p. 3; *Collected Poems*, p. 29.

13 Thomas Merton (private letter) to Edward Rice from Cuba.

14 *The Seven Storey Mountain*, p. 310.

15 *Thirty Poems*, p. 14; *Collected Poems*, p. 44.

16 Thomas Merton, *A Man in the Divided Sea* (New York, 1946), p. 18; *Collected Poems*, p. 63.

17 *A Man in the Divided Sea*, p. 31; *Collected Poems*, p. 73.

18 *A Man in the Divided Sea*, p. 18; *Collected Poems*, p. 74.

19 *Thirty Poems*, p. 7; *Collected Poems*, p. 35. Philip M. Stark, S.J., in "Two Poems to a Dead Brother: Catullus and Thomas Merton," *Classical Bulletin*, No. 38 (April 1962), pp. 81-83, points up striking

similarities and contrasts between Catullus' (*circa* 56 B.C.) noted elegy, "Multa per gentes. . . ." with its poignant final line "Atque in perpetuum, frater, ave atque vale," and Merton's "For My Brother: Reported Missing in Action, 1943."

20 *The Seven Storey Mountain*, p. 389.

21 Thomas Merton, Journal, February 1, 1942. One of seven salvaged pages of a novitiate Journal, the remainder of which Merton destroyed. See *The Seven Storey Mountain*, p. 310.

22 *A Man in the Divided Sea*, p. 57; *Collected Poems*, p. 93.

23 *Figures for an Apocalypse* (New York, 1947), pp. 13–28; *Collected Poems*, pp. 135–48.

24 *Figures for an Apocalypse*, p. 63; *Collected Poems*, p. 174.

25 *Figures for an Apocalypse*, p. 88; *Collected Poems*, p. 190.

26 *Figures for an Apocalypse*, p. 80; *Collected Poems*, p. 185.

27 *Figures for an Apocalypse*, pp. 88–90; *Collected Poems*, pp. 191–92.

28 Thomas Merton, Journal (March 7, 1948) (manuscript).

29 *Figures for an Apocalypse*, pp. 91–92; *Collected Poems*, pp. 192–93.

CHAPTER   TWO

1 Thomas Merton, *The Tears of the Blind Lions* (New York, 1949), p. 1; *Collected Poems*, p. 197.

2 *The Tears of the Blind Lions*, p. 24; *Collected Poems*, pp. 214–15.

3 *The Tears of the Blind Lions*, pp. 19–20; *Collected Poems*, pp. 209–10.

4 *The Tears of the Blind Lions*, pp. 15–18; *Collected Poems*, pp. 206–9.

5 *The Tears of the Blind Lions*, p. 5; *Collected Poems*, p. 198.

6 *The Tears of the Blind Lions*, p. 26; *Collected Poems*, p. 217.

7 *The Tears of the Blind Lions*, p. 27; *Collected Poems*, p. 218.

8 *The Tears of the Blind Lions*, pp. 28–29; *Collected Poems*, pp. 219–20.

9 *The Tears of the Blind Lions*, pp. 10–11; *Collected Poems*, pp. 202–3.

10 *The Tears of the Blind Lions*, p. 30; *Collected Poems*, p. 222.

11 Letter (November 3, 1958).

12 Letter (July 12, 1955).

13 Thomas Merton, *The Strange Islands* (New York, 1957), pp. 36–42; *Collected Poems*, pp. 239–45.

14 *The Strange Islands*, pp. 27–31; *Collected Poems*, pp. 232–36.

15 Thomas Merton, *The Tower of Babel (An Explanation)*, written at the request of those who were preparing a TV script of the drama for the "Catholic Hour." See Appendix.

16 *The Strange Islands*, "The Tower of Babel, A Morality," pp. 45–78; *Collected Poems*, pp. 247–73.

CHAPTER THREE

1 Thomas Merton, Notebook #70. Readings, etc. (1963).
2 Thomas Merton, *Emblems of a Season of Fury* (New York, 1963), pp. 4–5; *Collected Poems*, pp. 306–7.
3 *Emblems of a Season of Fury* p. 6; *Collected Poems*, p. 308.
4 *Emblems of a Season of Fury*, pp. 7–8; *Collected Poems*, pp. 309–10.
5 *Emblems of a Season of Fury*, p. 89; *Collected Poems*, p. 391.
6 *Emblems of a Season of Fury*, pp. 45, 47; *Collected Poems*, pp. 347, 349.
7 "Epitaph for a Public Servant, (In Memoriam—Adolf Eichmann)" (manuscript), p. 4; *Collected Poems*, pp. 710–11.
8 *Emblems of a Season of Fury*, pp. 54–57; *Collected Poems*, pp. 356–59.
9 Thomas Merton, holograph page explaining the genesis of the poem "Hagia Sophia." Merton adds: "Now the poem has been printed in a limited edition of some fifty copies by Victor Hammer on his press at the *Stamperia del Santuccio in Lexington*. This text has been mimeographed for the sake of those who might not have access to one of the printed copies.

"In an hour when madness seems to triumph over everything, let us remember that Wisdom is always victorious. The crown she has placed on the *Logos* is the crown of eternal kingship. 'For His power is an everlasting power and His Kingdom is to all generations' (Daniel 4:31)." The page is signed "T. M. January 1962." A note at bottom reads: "Since the monograph publication the poem has been reprinted in *Emblems of a Season of Fury* (1963)."
10 Thomas Merton (letter) to Victor Hammer, May 14, 1959, p. 1. (This is a carbon copy of the letter which Merton sent to the author of this study together with the manuscript of "Hagia Sophia.")
11 *Emblems of a Season of Fury*, pp. 61–69; *Collected Poems*, pp. 363–71.

CHAPTER FOUR

1 *Figures for an Apocalypse*, p. 72; *Collected Poems*, p. 180.
2 *The Tears of the Blind Lions*, pp. 30–31; *Collected Poems*, pp. 220–21.
3 In addition to "Wisdom in Emptiness: A Dialogue by Daisetz T. Suzuki and Thomas Merton," first published in *New Directions in Prose and Poetry 17* (New York, 1961) and reprinted in Thomas Merton's *Zen and the Birds of Appetite* (New York, 1968), in the spring of 1964, at Suzuki's request, Merton's superiors permitted him to travel to New York to meet the Zen master and confer with him. Of this meeting Merton records in his Journal for June 20, 1964:

"Suzuki likes Eckhart very much as I already know from the book of his that I got of the U. of K., several years ago.

"These conversations were certainly pleasant. It was profoundly important to me to see and experience the fact that there really is a deep understanding between myself and this extraordinary and simple man whose books I have been reading now for about ten years with great attention. I had a renewed sense of being 'situated' in this world. This is a legitimate consolation. . . . . . For once in a long time I felt as if I had spent a few moments with my own family."

4 *The Strange Islands*, p. 87; *Collected Poems*, p. 280.
5 *The Strange Islands*, p. 101; *Collected Poems*, pp. 289–90.
6 Thomas Merton, *Zen and the Birds of Appetite*, p. 71.
7 *The Strange Islands*, pp. 101–2; *Collected Poems*, p. 290.
8 Raymond Bernard Blakney, *Meister Eckhart* (New York and London, 1941), second edition, p. 232.
9 *The Strange Islands*, p. 86; *Collected Poems*, pp. 279–80.
10 *Zen and the Birds of Appetite*, p. 12.
11 *Cables to the Ace*, p. 58, No. 84; *Collected Poems*, p. 452.
12 *The Strange Islands*, p. 85; *Collected Poems*, p. 279.
13 *The Strange Islands*, p. 88; *Collected Poems*, p. 281.
14 *Zen and the Birds of Appetite*, p. 7.
15 *Emblems of a Season of Fury*, p. 52; *Collected Poems*, p. 354.
16 *Emblems of a Season of Fury*, pp. 47–49; *Collected Poems*, pp. 349–51.
17 *Emblems of a Season of Fury*, p. 51; *Collected Poems*, p. 353.
18 *Emblems of a Season of Fury*, p. 43; *Collected Poems*, pp. 344–45.
19 *Emblems of a Season of Fury*, p. 50; *Collected Poems*, pp. 351–52.
20 *Emblems of a Season of Fury*, pp. 38–39; *Collected Poems*, pp. 340–41.
21 *Emblems of a Season of Fury*, p. 52; *Collected Poems*, p. 354.
22 *Cables to the Ace*, p. 27, No. 38; *Collected Poems*, p. 421.
23 *Emblems of a Season of Fury*, pp. 35–36; *Collected Poems*, pp. 337–38.

CHAPTER   FIVE

1 *The Collected Poems of Thomas Merton* (New York, 1977).
2 "Paper Cranes" (manuscript), published in *Prelude 27* (1966); *Collected Poems*, p. 740.
3 Notebook #70: Readings, etc. (1963).
4 "Seneca"* (manuscript); shorter version in *Collected Poems*, pp. 619–20.
5 "Origen"* (manuscript); *Collected Poems*, pp. 640–41.
6 "St. Maedoc—Fragment of an Ikon," published as *Unicorn Broadsheet 7*; *Collected Poems*, pp. 752–53.
7 "With the World in my Blood Stream"* (manuscript); *Collected Poems*, pp. 615–18. The lines that refer to "My metal system/My invented backbone" relate to a vertebral fusion performed to correct a

deteriorated disc due to an old injury. (Letter, July 7, 1966).

8 "The Lion"* (manuscript); *Collected Poems,* p. 643.

9 "Early Blizzard" (manuscript); *Collected Poems,* pp. 650–51.

10 Rainer Maria Rilke, *Possibility of Being,* translated by J. B. Leishman (New York, 1977), p. 35.

11 "Rilke's Epitaph"* (manuscript); *Collected Poems,* p. 620.

12 "Le Secret"* (manuscript).

13 "The Night of Destiny"* (manuscript); *Collected Poems,* pp. 634–35.

14 Thomas Merton, "A Round and a Hope for Smithgirls" (manuscript); *Collected Poems,* pp. 678–79.

15 "The Originators"* (manuscript); *Collected Poems,* p. 613.

16 "A Carol" (manuscript); *Collected Poems,* pp. 649–50.

17 "Les Cinq Vièrges" (manuscript); *Collected Poems,* p. 819.

* Poems marked with an asterisk were originally intended for Part II of *Cables to the Ace,* then called "Edifying Cables."

CHAPTER SIX

1 Gerard Manley Hopkins, *Poems of Gerard Manley Hopkins,* (Mount Vernon, New York, n.d.), pp. 50–53.

2 Thomas Merton, Orientation Notes, (manuscript) Vol. VI, pp. 38–41, (December 1954–October 1955).

3 Hopkins, *op. cit.,* p. 52.

4 *The Collected Works of St. John of the Cross,* translated by Kieran Kavanaugh, O.C.D., and Otilio Rodriguez, O.C.D. (Washington, D.C., 1973), p. 117.

5 *Thirty Poems,* p. 16; *Collected Poems,* p. 46.

6 *A Man in the Divided Sea,* p. 64; *Collected Poems,* p. 98.

7 *Thirty Poems,* p. 16; *Collected Poems,* pp. 46–47.

8 *Thirty Poems,* p. 5; *Collected Poems,* pp. 32–33.

9 *A Man in the Divided Sea,* p. 20; *Collected Poems,* p. 65.

10 *A Man in the Divided Sea,* p. 20; *Collected Poems,* p. 83.

11 *Thirty Poems,* p. 13; *Collected Poems,* p. 44.

12 *The Tears of the Blind Lions,* pp. 8–9; *Collected Poems,* pp. 200–1.

13 *The Tears of the Blind Lions,* p. 27; *Collected Poems,* p. 219.

14 *The Strange Islands,* pp. 93–94; *Collected Poems,* p. 284.

15 *Thirty Poems,* p. 23; *Collected Poems,* pp. 55–56.

16 *A Man in the Divided Sea,* p. 51; *Collected Poems,* p. 88.

17 *A Man in the Divided Sea,* p. 52; *Collected Poems,* p. 89.

18 *A Man in the Divided Sea,* p. 70; *Collected Poems,* pp. 102–3.

19 *Figures for an Apocalypse,* p. 79; *Collected Poems,* p. 185.

20 *Thirty Poems,* p. 9; *Collected Poems,* p. 38.

21 *Thirty Poems,* p. 7; *Collected Poems,* p. 35.

22 *Thirty Poems,* p. 12; *Collected Poems,* pp. 40–41.

23 *A Man in the Divided Sea,* p. 42; *Collected Poems,* pp. 82–83.

24 Grace Sisson, daughter of Elbert Sisson of Bryan's Road, Maryland.

25 *Emblems of a Season of Fury,* pp. 28–29; *Collected Poems,* pp. 330–31.

26 *Emblems of a Season of Fury,* pp. 20–22; *Collected Poems,* pp. 323–24.

27 "Picture of a Black Child with a White Doll (Carole Denise McNair, killed in Birmingham, September 1963)" (manuscript); *Collected Poems,* pp. 626–27.

28 *Emblems of a Season of Fury,* pp. 30–32; *Collected Poems,* pp. 332–34.

29 *A Man in the Divided Sea,* pp. 89–91; *Collected Poems,* pp. 116–18.

30 *The Strange Islands,* preface.

31 *Selected Poems,* with an introduction by Mark Van Doren (Enlarged Edition: New York, 1967), p. xi.

32 *The Strange Islands,* pp. 99–100; *Collected Poems,* pp. 288–89.

33 William J. Lynch, *Christ and Apollo* (New York, 1960), pp. 192, 193.

34 *Emblems of a Season of Fury,* pp. 23–27; *Collected Poems,* pp. 325–29.

35 *Emblems of a Season of Fury,* pp. 13–14; *Collected Poems,* pp. 315–16.

36 *Emblems of a Season of Fury,* p. 14; *Collected Poems,* p. 316.

37 *Emblems of a Season of Fury,* pp. 8–9; *Collected Poems,* pp. 310–11.

38 "Elegy for Father Stephen" (manuscript); included in *Collected Poems,* pp. 631–32, as "Elegy for a Trappist."

39 "Hymn of Not Much Praise for New York City" (manuscript); *Collected Poems,* p. 21.

40 *Figures for an Apocalypse,* p. 23; *Collected Poems,* p. 144.

41 *Emblems of a Season of Fury,* p. 6; *Collected Poems,* p. 309.

42 *The Strange Islands,* p. 19; *Collected Poems,* p. 221.

43 Thomas Merton, "Answers for H. Lavin Gerda" (manuscript), p. 2.

44 "First Lesson About Man" (manuscript); *Collected Poems,* pp. 624–26.

45 *The Strange Islands,* p. 66; *Collected Poems,* p. 263.

CHAPTER   SEVEN

1 Thomas Merton (letter), September 1966.

2 Thomas Merton, Notebook #79 (April–June 1966).

3 Thomas Merton, "Writing as Temperature" (September 1968) (manuscript), p. 8.

4 Thomas Merton, "Author's Note" to *The Geography of Lograire* (New York, 1969), p. 1; *Collected Poems,* p. 457.

5 André Breton, *Manifestoes of Surrealism* (Ann Arbor, Michigan, 1969), pp. 36–37.

6 *Cables to the Ace,* No. 14, pp. 9–10; *Collected Poems,* pp. 403–4.

7 Thomas Merton, Notebook-Cables #75 (1965–1966).

8 Ibid.

9 *Cables to the Ace,* Nos. 5, 6, 13, 15, 16, 17, 22, 25, 26, 27, 28, 29, 34, 41, 42, 45, 47, 53, 54, 55, 56, 57, 58, 59. Nos. 60, 61, 70, 78, and 88 were added to the 1967 manuscript; these were not included in the 1966 mss. Nos. 44, 46, 48, 66, and 82 were likewise added to the 1967 manuscript, but copied out of the *Cables* working notebook. Nos. 19, 35, 36, 37, 38, 40, 62, 63, 64, 65, 67, 68, 69, 73, 84, 85, 86, and "Prologue" were added after the 1967 manuscript.

10 *Cables to the Ace,* No. 6, p. 4; *Collected Poems,* p. 398.

11 Thomas Merton, "Terror and the Absurd—Violence and Non-violence in Albert Camus" (August 1966); "Camus and the Catholic Church" (August 1966); "Three Saviors" (September 1966); and "The Stranger: Poverty of an Anti-Hero" (March 1968).

12 Thomas Merton, "Edifying Cables" (manuscript, 1966), p. 1. This section was also included in the 1967 manuscript, in the printed text, 1968, p. 3, and in the *Collected Poems,* p. 397.

13 *Cables to the Ace,* No. 33, p. 23; *Collected Poems,* p. 417.

14 *Cables to the Ace,* No. 34, p. 24; *Collected Poems,* p. 418.

15 *Cables to the Ace,* No. 48, p. 33; *Collected Poems,* p. 427.

16 *Cables to the Ace,* No. 5, p. 4; *Collected Poems,* p. 398.

17 *Cables to the Ace,* No. 15, p. 10; *Collected Poems,* p. 404.

18 *Cables to the Ace,* No. 16, p. 11; *Collected Poems,* p. 405.

19 *Cables to the Ace,* No. 22, p. 17; *Collected Poems,* p. 411.

20 *Cables to the Ace,* No. 44, p. 30; *Collected Poems,* p. 424.

21 *Cables to the Ace,* No. 18, p. 13; *Collected Poems,* p. 407.

22 *Cables to the Ace,* No. 14, p. 9; *Collected Poems,* p. 403.

23 *Cables to the Ace,* No. 82, p. 56; *Collected Poems,* p. 450. The dove descending into the "center of the vision" has a corresponding symbolic passage in T. S. Eliot's "Little Gidding" (*Four Quartets*), in which "The dove descending breaks the air/With flame of incandescent terror," both passages occuring at the mystical high point of the respective poems.

24 *Cables to the Ace,* No. 83, p. 17; *Collected Poems,* p. 451.

25 *Cables to the Ace,* No. 35, p. 26; *Collected Poems,* p. 420.

26 *Cables to the Ace,* No. 37, p. 27; *Collected Poems,* p. 421.

27 *Cables to the Ace,* No. 38, p. 27; *Collected Poems,* p. 421.

28 *Cables to the Ace,* No. 84, p. 58; *Collected Poems,* p. 452.

29 *Emblems of a Season of Fury,* p. 52; *Collected Poems,* p. 354.

30 *Cables to the Ace,* No. 87, p. 59; *Collected Poems,* p. 453.

31 *Zen and the Birds of Appetite,* pp. 11–12.

32 *Cables to the Ace,* No. 70, p. 50; *Collected Poems,* p. 444.

33 *Cables to the Ace*, No. 74, p. 51; *Collected Poems*, p. 445.

34 *Cables to the Ace*, No. 34, p. 24; *Collected Poems*, p. 418.

35 *Cables to the Ace*, No. 80, p. 55; *Collected Poems*, p. 449.

36 *Thirty Poems*, p. 5; *Collected Poems*, p. 33.

37 *Cables to the Ace*, No. 84, p. 55; *Collected Poems*, p. 449.

38 *Cables to the Ace*, No. 45, p. 31; *Collected Poems*, p. 425.

39 Notebook #79 (April–June 1966).

40 *Virginia Quarterly Review* (Summer 1968).

41 Thomas Merton, "The Monastic Theology of St. Aelred," preface to a book by A. Hallier (September 1968) (manuscript), p. 6.

42 *Cables to the Ace*, No. 78, p. 54; *Collected Poems*, p. 449.

CHAPTER   EIGHT

1 Thomas Merton, *The Geography of Lograire*, cover page of manuscript. Text from Gaston Bachelard, translated; "To render language unpredictable, is it not an apprenticeship of liberty?"

2 Ibid., p. 1.

3 Ibid.

4 Ibid.

5 Ibid., p. 2.

6 Ibid., pp. 6–10.

7 Francois René Chateaubriand, translated: "Each man carries within him a world made up of all that he has seen and loved, and to which he continually returns, even though he travels and appears to live in a foreign world."

8 *The Geography of Lograire*, (New York, 1968), p. 4; *Collected Poems*, p. 460.

9 *The Geography of Lograire*, p. 4; *Collected Poems*, p. 460.

10 *The Seven Storey Mountain*, p. 101.

11 *The Geography of Lograire*, p. 4; *Collected Poems*, p. 460.

12 *The Geography of Lograire*, p. 5; *Collected Poems*, p. 461.

13 Thomas Merton, *Conjectures of a Guilty Bystander* (New York, 1966), pp. 181–82.

14 *The Geography of Lograire*, p. 12; *Collected Poems*, p. 468.

15 *The Geography of Lograire*, p. 27; *Collected Poems*, p. 483.

16 *The Geography of Lograire*, pp. 28–30; *Collected Poems*, pp. 484–86.

17 *The Geography of Lograire*, p. 22; *Collected Poems*, p. 478.

18 *The Geography of Lograire*, p. 44; *Collected Poems*, p. 500.

19 *The Geography of Lograire*, p. 47; *Collected Poems*, p. 503.

20 *The Geography of Lograire*, pp. 41–42; *Collected Poems*, pp. 497–98.

21 *The Geography of Lograire*, p. 54; *Collected Poems*, p. 510.

22 *The Geography of Lograire*, p. 60; *Collected Poems*, p. 516.

23 *The Geography of Lograire*, (manuscript), p. 23.

24 *The Geography of Lograire*, p. 62; *Collected Poems*, p. 518.

25 *The Geography of Lograire*, pp. 71–72, 76; *Collected Poems*, pp. 525, 527–28, 532.

26 *The Geography of Lograire*, p. 148; *Collected Poems*, p. 604.

27 *The Geography of Lograire*, p. 100; *Collected Poems*, p. 556.

28 *The Geography of Lograire*, p. 104; *Collected Poems*, p. 560.

29 *The Geography of Lograire*, pp. 115, 116; *Collected Poems*, pp. 571, 572.

30 *The Geography of Lograire*, pp. 119–26; *Collected Poems*, pp. 575–81.

31 *The Geography of Lograire*, pp. 127–30; *Collected Poems*, pp. 583–86.

32 *The Geography of Lograire*, p. 131; *Collected Poems*, p. 587.

33 *The Geography of Lograire*, pp. 132, 133, 134–35; *Collected Poems*, pp. 588, 589, 590–91.

CHAPTER NINE

1 Thomas Merton, "Poetry and Contemplation: A Reappraisal," *Selected Poems*, (New York, 1959), pp. 107–35.

2 Thomas Merton, "Graph of My Work" (manuscript).

3 "Dirge for the World Joyce Died In" (manuscript); *Collected Poems*, p. 4.

4 "Two British Airmen (Buried with ceremony in the Teutoburg Forest)" (manuscript); *Collected Poems*, p. 5.

5 "The Strife Between the Poet and Ambition" (manuscript); *Collected Poems*, p. 11.

6 *Collected Poems*, pp. 1017–30.

7 *The Asian Journal of Thomas Merton* (New York, 1973), pp. 222–28; *Collected Poems*, pp. 715–21.

8 *Cables to the Ace*, back cover.

9 Thomas Merton, "Why Alienation Is for Everybody" (manuscript).

10 *The Geography of Lograire*, p. 123; *Collected Poems*, p. 579.

11 *Selected Poems* (1959), p. 108.

12 *Emblems of a Season of Fury*, p. 35; *Collected Poems*, p. 337.

13 Thomas Merton, *Bread in the Wilderness* (New York, 1953), pp. 54–55.

14 "Antipoem I" (Notebook #74, 1964); *Collected Poems*, pp. 671–72.

15 "Message to Poets" (February 1964), p. 3.

16 Sister Thérèse Lentfoehr, "Out of a Cloud," *America* (Vol. 121, No. 20, December 1969), p. 585.

17 Thomas Merton, Letter to Aldous Huxley, (February 27, 1958) (manuscript), p. 3.

18 Daniel Berrigan, S.J., "Funeral Oration for Thomas Merton as Spoken by the Compassionate Buddha" (manuscript), p. 2.

The Tower of Babel: An Explanation

The Theme: The basic idea of this philosophic "morality play" is *the unity of man in the charity and truth of Christ.*

Man is made in the image of God. That is to say he is made to be united to God and to his fellow man in the sharing of a common vision of God's truth. This is his true destiny, and in this alone can he be truly happy.

No man can come to perfect happiness by himself. Our salvation is a corporate work: we learn the truth from one another, and we help one another to grow in likeness to God by charity. But for this corporate work of our salvation to take place, we depend on the use of a divinely given instrument: language.

The builders of the Tower of Babel are men who have repudiated God and His Truth. Instead of using their divinely given endowments in the service of God, they pervert His creatures and themselves by turning all things to the worship of themselves. The Tower is the symbol of man's pride and self-sufficiency without God. The building of the Tower is man's worship of his own technological skill, of his own wealth, his own ambitions, his own power to crush other men and make them his slaves. The building of the Tower of Babel is man's construction of the great illusion that he himself is a god. This is the illusion which lies at the root of all the evils of our time.

Man's true destiny is to build another city—the city of love, and not the city of pride. This city of love is the city of God. St.

Augustine long ago contrasted the two cities, Babylon and Jerusalem, saying: "These two cities are built by two loves: the first by love of self unto the contempt of God, the second by love of God unto the contempt of self." But the city of love is the Church, the Mystical Body of Christ, and it is built by those who, renouncing themselves and their illusory pride, love God with their whole heart and love their neighbor as themselves. These are they who, united in Christ, have the truth dwelling in their hearts and manifest it in the darkness of the world of sin.

Part 1—scene 1—*Building the Tower*—The apparent unity of the builders in their common purpose is an illusion. The apparent strength of the great tower is only a shadow. Man's pride remakes the world on a foundation of pure falsity. That falsity must inevitably break through, and the world of illusion must collapse. Meanwhile, in order to preserve the illusion, three great means are used: a frantic activism, the domination of the masses by fear, and ultimately the use of violence, in war. All these means must fail. The structure must inevitably fall to the ground.

Part 1—scene 2—*The Trial*. The fall of the tower does not cure man of his illusion. On the contrary, by means of war, lying propaganda, and false philosophies, the illusion is spread abroad and carried to the ends of the earth. All men become infected by it. The Leader of Babel puts Truth and Language on trial for their life. That is, he claims the right to manipulate the truth and to make words mean what he pleases. To the men of Babel words are only justified in so far as they can be made to serve the great illusion. But the very nature of language is to bear witness to objective truth: and this objective truth is the enemy of the great illusion. Ultimately, the men of Babel are forced to use thought, words, and ideologies in order to destroy all meaning and to keep men from getting in contact with one another and living in unity. Materialistic society is doomed to disintegration and will ultimately collapse.

Part 2—scene 1—*Zodiac*. In this scene, lyrical and reflective, we meditate on the nature of men, on his need for unity, and on the fact that this unity cannot be achieved unless men can communicate the truth to one another. But for men to be united in the truth, God Himself must intervene, sending into the world His Word, that is His own Truth, in the person of Christ. Men will ultimately find unity and peace only when they are united in Christ.

Part 2—scene 2—*The Exiles*. Lonely and disoriented, the victims of Babel wander aimlessly in a wasteland, wondering if life can have any meaning. The Prophet finds them and tells them they must hope for a solution, and seek it with all their power. Life does indeed have meaning. Man's thought, and art, and work, and social living can indeed become fruitful and happy once again, since they have been purified of the great illusion. God will send Christ, His Son, Who will redeem man and purify his soul and make him ready to receive the light. United in the light of Christ, man will once again discover unity, and fruitfulness, and joy (The Village Festival). The world is not evil, and man's city is not itself an illusion. Only Babel is illusion. Man's society united in the peace of Christ, reflects the great ultimate reality of God Himself and foreshadows our destiny to be eternally one in Him. When this has been made clear, the Fall of Babylon is heard: this time the definite fall, that marks the end of time and the final victory of Christ in His Church. The play ends with exaltation of the Church acclaiming the victory of truth over falsity, and reviewing the whole history of salvation: the action of God's Truth in the darkness of falsity and sin.

THOMAS MERTON

BIBLIOGRAPHY

Books by Thomas Merton

POETRY

Thirty Poems. New York: New Directions, 1944.
A Man in the Divided Sea. New York: New Directions, 1946.
Figures for an Apocalypse. New York: New Directions, 1947.
Tears of the Blind Lions. New York: New Directions, 1949.
The Strange Islands. New York: New Directions, 1957.
Selected Poems. Introductions by Mark Van Doren. New York: New Directions, 1959.
Hagia Sophia. Lexington, Kentucky: Stamperia del Santuccio, Op. 17, No. 64, 1962.
Emblems of a Season of Fury. New York: New Directions, 1963.
Selected Poems. Enlarged Edition. New York: New Directions, 1967.
Cables to the Ace. New York: New Directions, 1968.
The Geography of Lograire. New York: New Directions, 1969.
Early Poems/1940-42. Lexington, Kentucky: The Anvil Press, 1971.
The Collected Poems of Thomas Merton. New York: New Directions, 1977.

SELECTED PROSE

The Seven Storey Mountain. New York: Harcourt Brace, 1948.
Seeds of Contemplation. New York: New Directions, 1949.
Bread in the Wilderness. New York: New Directions, 1953.
The Sign of Jonas. New York: Harcourt Brace, 1953.
No Man is an Island. New York: Farrar, Straus & Cudahy, 1957.
The Silent Life. New York: Farrar, Straus & Cudahy, 1957.
Thoughts in Solitude. New York: Farrar, Straus & Cudahy, 1958.
The Tower of Babel. Norfolk, Connecticut: New Directions, 1958.
The Wisdom of the Desert. New York: New Directions, 1960.

The Way of Chuang Tzu. New York: New Directions, 1965.
Conjectures of a Guilty Bystander. New York: Doubleday, 1966.
Zen and the Birds of Appetite. New York: New Directions, 1968.
New Seeds of Contemplation. New York: New Directions, 1972.
The Asian Journal of Thomas Merton. New York: New Directions, 1973.

MANUSCRIPTS

The manuscripts listed below are in the author's collection (sent to her through the years by Thomas Merton), with the exception of Tom's Book, and Notebooks #70, #74, #75, and #79, from which brief quotations have been taken; they were made available at the Thomas Merton Studies Center, Louisville, Kentucky, through the courtesy of James Laughlin, publisher of New Directions and chairman of the Merton Legacy Trust.

Answers to H. Lavin Gerda. For *Punto Final,* Chile, 1967.
"Edifying Cables." 1966 and 1967 versions of *Cables to the Ace.*
The Geography of Lograire. Notebook. (Xeroxed copy made available to the author through the courtesy of James Laughlin.)
Graph of My Work.
Hagia Sophia. Early drafts, including letter to Victor Hammer dated May 14, 1959, explaining the first draft.
Journal (December 1941–February 1942). "Salvaged pages"; cf. *Seven Storey Mountain,* page 389.
Journal (March 8, 1947–October 10, 1948).
Journal (June 20, 1964–September 1, 1965).
Letter to the author (July 12, 1955).
Letter to Ed Rice from Cuba (spring 1940).
Message to Poets (February 1964).
Monastic Orientation (Vol. VI, December 1954–October 1955).
Monastic Theology of St. Aelred (Preface to Book by A. Hallier, Sept. 1968).
Notebooks. #70 (Readings 1963), #74, #75 (1965–66) *Cables,* #79 (April–June 1966).
Terror and the Absurd. Violence and Non-Violence in Albert Camus (August 1966); "Camus and the Catholic Church" (August 1966); "Three Saviors" (September 1966); and "The Stranger: Poverty of an Anti-Hero" (March 1968).
Tom's Book (1915–16). Diary by Ruth Merton.
The Tower of Babel: An Explanation. Written at the request of those who were preparing a TV script of the verse drama for the "Catholic Hour."
Why Alienation Is for Everybody.

Writing as Temperature. Review of Roland Barthes' *Writing Degree Zero,* for *Sewanee Review,* Vol. LXXXII, No. 3 (July–September 1969).

POEMS IN MANUSCRIPT

The following poems were sent to the author by Thomas Merton in the summer of 1967, together with the 1967 manuscript of "Edifying Cables," (later called *Cables to the Ace*), for which they had been originally intended as Part II. All these poems now appear in *The Collected Poems of Thomas Merton.* Pages are noted.

"With the World in my Blood Stream," p. 615.
"A Baroque Gravure (From a 17th Century Book of Piety)", p. 618.
"Seneca," p. 619.
"The Prospects of Nostradamus" (later added to *Cables to the Ace*), p. 437.
"Rilke's Epitaph," p. 620.
"Reading Translated Poets, Feb. 1," p. 621.
"The Great Men of Former Times," p. 623.
"First Lesson About Man," p. 624.
"Picture of a Black Child with a White Doll (Carole Denise McNair killed in Birmingham, Sept. 1963)," p. 626.
"Tonight There Is a Showing of Champion Lights," p. 628.
"Sensation Time at the Home," p. 629 (under the title of "A Song: Sensation Time at the Home").
"Elegy for a Trappist," p. 631.
"A Tune for Festive Dances in the Nineteen Sixties," p. 632.
"The Night of Destiny," p. 634.
"Le Secret," p. 635.
"Man the Master," p. 637.
"Origen," p. 640.
"For the Spanish Poet Miguel Hernandez," p. 641.
"The Lion," p. 643.
"Fall '66—*Arturum etiam sub terris bella moventem,*" p. 644.
"Hopeless and Felons," p. 647.
"Long Enough," p. 726.

To this group of late poems, James Laughlin added manuscripts of the following—now also published in the *Collected Poems.*

"The Originators," p. 613.
"A Carol," p. 649.
"Lubnan," p. 614.

"Early Blizzard," p. 650.

"You Are About to Be Surprised" (later called, "Miami, You Are About to
 Be Surprised" and appearing in *The Geography of Lograire*), p. 473.

"Why I Have a Wet Footprint on Top of My Mind," p. 497.

"Welcome," p. 646.

"Plessy vs Ferguson: Theme and Variations," p. 651.

"Ben's Last Fight," p. 661.

"Rites for the Extrusion of a Leper," p. 655.

To these two groups of late poems, Naomi Burton Stone added "St.
Maedoc—Fragment of an Ikon," p. 752.

In the last four years or so before his death, Merton sent the author
manuscripts of the following poems, now published in *Collected Poems*.
Pages are noted.

"Epitaph for a Public Servant (*In Memoriam—Adolf Eichman*)," p. 703.

"Newscast" (later incorporated into *Cables to the Ace*), p. 427.

"Prayer to Saint Anatole" (later incorporated into *Cables to the Ace*),
 p. 425.

"Western Fellow Students Salute with Calypso Anthems the Movie Career
 of Robert Lax," p. 811.

"A Round and a Hope for Smithgirls," p. 678.

"Les Cinq Vierges," p. 819.

"The Great Men of Former Times," p. 623.

"A Song from the Geography of Lograire" (under "South," I, "Will a
 narrow lane/Save Cain?"), p. 465.

"Paper Cranes (The Hibakusha Come to Gethsemani)," p. 740.

INDEX